POETRY

GREAT MINDS

Your World...Your Future...YOUR WORDS

- Moving On
Edited by Steve Twelvetree

Young Writers

First published in Great Britain in 2005 by:
Young Writers
Remus House
Coltsfoot Drive
Peterborough
PE2 9JX
Telephone: 01733 890066
Website: www.youngwriters.co.uk

All Rights Reserved

© *Copyright Contributors 2005*

SB ISBN 1 84602 297 5

Foreword

This year, the Young Writers' 'Great Minds' competition proudly presents a showcase of the best poetic talent selected from over 40,000 up-and-coming writers nationwide.

Young Writers was established in 1991 to promote the reading and writing of poetry within schools and to the youth of today. Our books nurture and inspire confidence in the ability of young writers and provide a snapshot of poems written in schools and at home by budding poets of the future.

The thought, effort, imagination and hard work put into each poem impressed us all and the task of selecting poems was a difficult but nevertheless enjoyable experience.

We hope you are as pleased as we are with the final selection and that you and your family continue to be entertained with *Great Minds - Moving On* for many years to come.

Contents

Bideford College, Bideford
Laura Atkinson (14) — 1
Clare Penny (14) — 2
Emma Wilson (14) — 3
Leah Jeffery (14) — 4
Ruby Hudson — 5

Carmel Technology College, Darlington
Adam Bowman (14) — 5
Liam Coates (14) — 6
Charlotte McAuley (14) — 6
Gabrielle McKenna (13) — 7
Emma Galbraith (12) — 7
Liam Campbell (13) — 8
Amy Raper (12) — 8
Sean Kelly (13) — 9
James Smith (13) — 9
Stephanie Spence (13) — 10
Emma Hird (13) — 10
Jonathan Lumsdon (13) — 11
Dillon Zhou (12) — 11
Elizabeth Sutcliffe (14) — 12
Lewis Brown (12) — 13
Gavin Rodgers (14) — 14
Philip Massingham (12) — 14
Andrew James Clifford (13) — 15
Jessica Wake (13) — 15
Rachel Musgrave (13) — 16
Thomas Haile (14) — 17
Hannah Pritchard (13) — 18
Kieren Kemp (14) — 18
Emma Bantleman (14) — 19
Patrick Wharton (14) — 19
Jessica Conway (14) — 20
Rebecca Eldrington (14) — 21
Katie Oxley (14) — 22
Sophie Mackay (14) — 23
Adam Bell (14) — 24
Sadie McCartney (13) — 24

Sinead Wisker (14)	25
Laura Myers (12)	25
William Jones (14)	26
Abbi Fluen (14)	26
Victoria McAfee (15)	27
Daryl King (14)	27
Alisha Sinha (14)	28
Christopher Thomas Ward (13)	28
Ross Kelly (14)	29
Luke Williamson (14)	29
Stephanie Metcalfe (13)	30
Ben Foster (12)	31
Richard McAllister (13)	32
Rebecca King (12)	32
Andrew Jordan (13)	33
Abby Clarke (13)	33
Rachel Baines (12)	34
Nicola Bleasby (13)	34
Paul McDermott (12)	35
Sarah McDonogh (15)	35
Stacey Marie Clegg (14)	36
Rachael Peeke (14)	36
Neil Hanlon (12)	37
Jack Meredith (15)	37
Kyrie J Hunter (15)	38
Kathryn Hall (15)	38
Jonathan Way (15)	39
Natasha Redpath (13)	39
Emma Spraggon (12)	40
Christopher Clinton (15)	40
Michael Thurloway (13)	41
Christina Muller (13)	41
Bethany Harper (12)	42
Louise Sowerby (12)	42
Thomas Wilson (12)	43
James Potts (11)	44

Eastbourne Secondary School, Darlington

Hollie McLean (11)	44
Declan Franklin (13)	45
Jennifer Hinde (12)	45

Simon Kieran (13)   45
Declan Gregory (12)   46

Eston Park School, Eston
Sarah Hardy (15)   46
Chun Chi Yau (15)   47
Joseph Dollery (13)   48
Emma Dawson (11)   48
Hayley Roxby-Allan (13)   49
Louise Johnston (15)   49
Kate Louise Stephenson (12)   50
Carl James (15)   51
Laura Cooke   51
Peter Lunn (14)   52
Jodie Fisher (15)   52
Daniel Hutchins (15)   53
Ainsley Lancaster (15)   54
Laura Allen (15)   54
Rebecca McNeil (15)   55
Lucinda Youngs (15)   55
Lindsay Robertson (15)   56
Amy McBride (15)   56
Sam Rudd (15)   57

Estover Community College, Estover
Robert Carter (13)   57
Danny Walton (13)   58
Jemma Rose (13)   59
Amy Mouncher (13)   60
Jade Pindard (13)   60
Nathan Reed (13)   61
Sammy-Jo Richards (13)   61
Rhys Hooper (13)   62
Becky Atkins (13)   62
Gemma Tully (13)   63

Highcliffe School, Christchurch
Joe Sherred (13)   63
Jenny Higson (11)   64
Charles Sugden   64

Elizabeth McDonald (14)	65
Gabriella-Rose Cooper (14)	66
Nicola-Jayne Hazzard (14)	66
Tom Griffiths (14)	67
Emily Millar (14)	67
Christopher Symons (14)	68
Leanne Stretton (14)	68
Michael Albin	69
Ellie Stanton (14)	69
Lucy Etheridge (15)	70
Heather Moult (14)	71
Sarah Di Battista (14)	72
Emma Cardus (14)	72
Lauren Cooper (12)	73

Lewis School Pengam, Gilfach

Samuel Griffiths (12)	73
Josh Joshua (12)	74
Joseph Leach (12)	75
Ashley Court (11)	76
Sam Forrest (12)	76
Alex Williams (13)	77
Gareth Griffiths (12)	78
Ben Clark (12)	78
David Shenton (12)	79
Nathan Hazell (12)	79
Rhys Owens (12)	80
Lee Knicz (12)	80
Matthew Powell (12)	81
Blake Edwards (12)	81
Jake Elliott (12)	82
Adam Vile (12)	83
Amar Ali (11)	83
Liam Shaughnessy (12)	84
Ben Rees (12)	84
Calum Duncan (12)	85

Penryn College, Penryn

Lizzie Clark (12)	85
Sancha Annear (12)	86
Gabby Moore (13)	87

Hal Parsons (13) 88
Cat Dove (13) 89

Radyr Comprehensive School, Cardiff
Louis Assiratti (12) 89
Matthew Learoyd (12) 90
Matthew Smith (12) 91
Alex Coombes (12) 91
Kim Howcroft (13) 92
Marc Tilley (12) 92
Amy Wiggins (12) 93
Sara Howell (12) 94
Huw Lewis (12) 95
Emily Donnan (12) 96
Olivia Beere (11) 96
Guy Howcroft (13) 97
Loren Evans (12) 97
Natasha Shorte (13) 98
Eleanor Baxter (12) 98
Louise Edmunds (13) 99
Hannah Manley (12) 99
Charlotte Rees (13) 100
Tom Heyman (11) 100
Arran Coe (13) 101
Rhys Laskey (13) 101
Ali Emad Jaffery (13) 102
Jared Hughes (13) 102
Sallyann Moore (13) 103
Amy Jenkins (13) 104
Lewis Jones (13) 105
Megan Burford (13) 105
Rhiannon Jones (14) 106
James Longville (13) 106
Rebekah Ellis (13) 107
Sam Lyle (13) 107
Megan Price (13) 108
Lewis Simpson (13) 108
Charlene Simmonds (14) 109
Kristian Matthews (13) 109
Jemma Flynn (14) 110
Daryl Murray (14) 110

Sam Langford (14)	111
Themis Zafiropoulos (14)	111
Ceri James (14)	112
Rowan Axe (14)	112
Mercedes Ttophi (14)	113
Katie Haskell (14)	113
Ryan Jenkins (12)	114
Sean McGrath (14)	114
Stacie Nicholls (14)	115
Claire Richards (13)	115
Yeats Yeung (12)	116
Lucy Robins (12)	117
Robbie Scott (11)	117
Christina Sueref (12)	118
Adam Mackinnon (14)	118
Hannah Bainbridge (12)	119
Ida Hennius (14)	119
Eluned Hyde (12)	120
David O'Connor (14)	120
Adam Heavens (12)	121
Daniel Coombes (13)	121
Sophia Homayoonfar (12)	122
Ben Liguz (12)	122
David Walker (12)	123
Ashley Blair (12)	123
Jessica Johns (12)	124
Ellis Hodgson (12)	124
Beckie Drew (13)	125
Rebecca Miller (13)	126
Gaël Shaw (14)	126
Ben Montgomery & Jordan Osman (12)	127
Alan Newton (12)	127
Lewis Hydes (13)	128
Jack Shellard (12)	128

St Colombans College, Kilkeel
Susie Reilly (11)	129

St Hild's CE School, Hartlepool
Alex Bainbridge (13)	130
Faye Whitehead	130

Rachel Bell	131
Emily Winter (12)	131
Sarah Coward	132
Rachel Laybourn	132
Liam Gray (13)	133
Emma Pounder (13)	133
Robbie Wood (13)	134
Sophie Austwicke	134
Andrew Townsend	135
Laura Blackett	135
Mark Austwicke (13)	136
Natalie Mathieson	136

St Luke's Science & Sports College, Exeter
Rob Shearman (13)	137

The Atherley School, Southampton
Jess Lind (12)	137

The Ladies' College, St Peter Port
Annaliese McGeoch (12)	138
Katie Enevoldsen (11)	138
Lorna Whattam (14)	139
Elizabeth Moffatt (14)	139
Joanna Woodnutt (13)	140
Alice Monaghan (13)	141
Kate Smith (13)	142
Ebby Mosgrove (13)	142
Issey Norman-Ross (12)	143
Tanith Cherry (12)	143
Bella Chesney (12)	144
Niamh Hanna (12)	144
Chantal Marson (13)	145

The Lakes School, Windermere
Alesha Solomon (12)	146
Robert Griffiths (12)	146
Matthew Park (12)	146
Annie Garlick (11)	147
Eilish Heatley	148

Tom Simmonds (12)	148
Christopher Hunter Marsh (12)	149
Rachel Pickup (14)	149
Will Britton (12)	150
Daniel Laffin (12)	150
Ellie McKeown (14)	151
Stephen Gibson (12)	152
Brandon Williamson (11)	152

Torquay Grammar School For Girls, Torquay

Holli Baker (15)	153

Wareham Middle School, Wareham

Elliot Journeaux (12)	154
Shannon Burbidge (10)	154
Geoffrey Dragon (13)	155
Paige Wallace (10)	155
Declan Walmsley (13)	156
Connor Gordon (10)	156
Jessica-Rose Clark (13)	157
Eleanor Wallace (13)	158
Amy Derrick (12)	159
Emily Rudd (13)	159
Kiri Snell (13)	160
Becky Fooks (12)	160
David Iles (12)	161
Glen Strowbridge (12)	162
Tom McConnell (12)	162
Alex Lane (10)	162
Joseph Lillington (13)	163
Josh Terrar (10)	163
Chris Cullinane (13)	164

The Poems

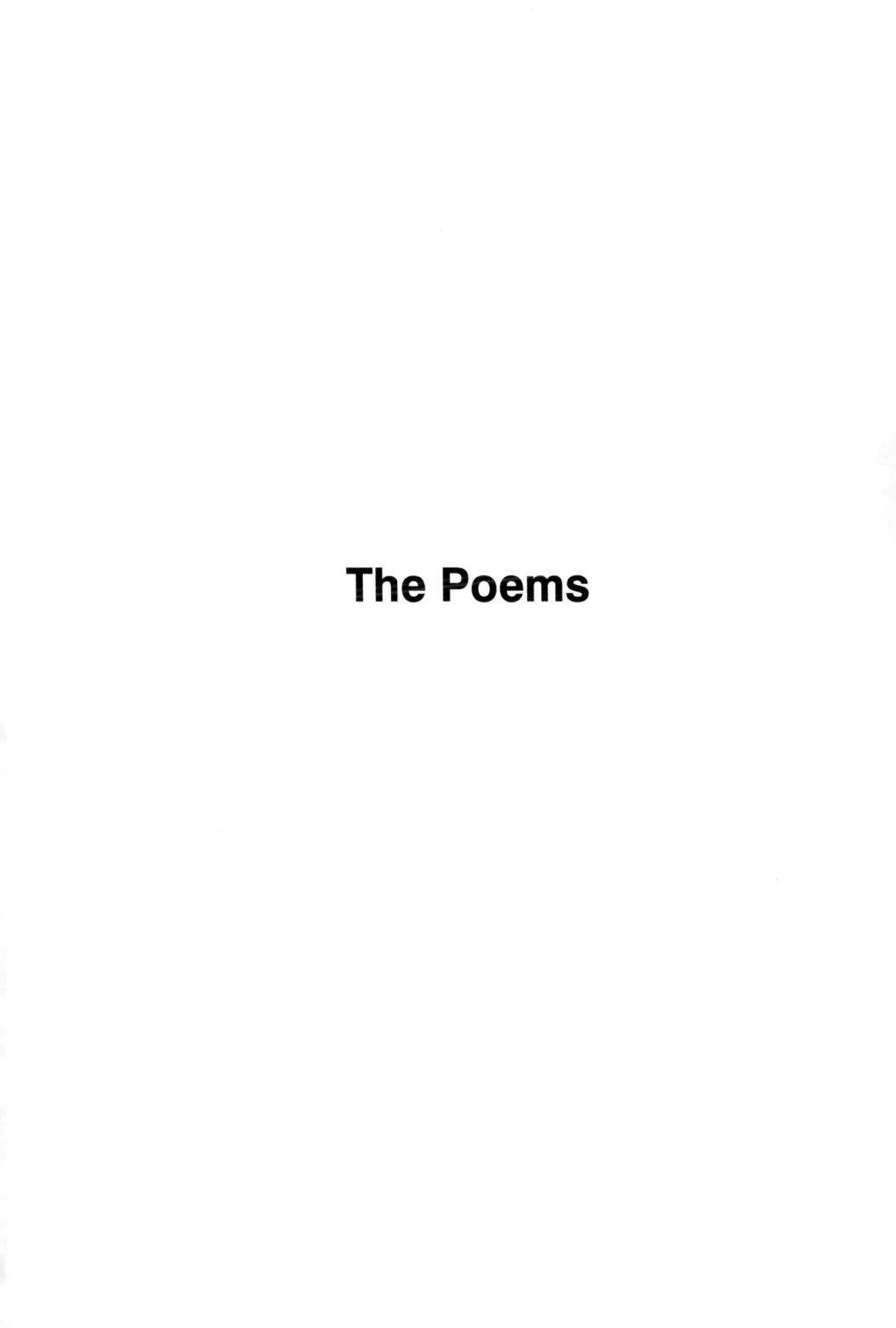

War

Breathless,
I lay forlorn longing to escape.
With a scarcely lit lamp I lay writing to my loved ones,
Bloodstained rags lay strewn around me,
With a gangrene foot and a rickety back, I lay in pain and remorse
I was hidden in the depths of my own self-pity.

Once again sunrise would form,
And the radiant sunbeams would scorch our backs,
We'd trudge through the grunge and mud,
To perform our duties and honour thy country.
Bang, bang! went the sound of the rifles searing through the air,
'Attention,' boomed the voice of our Sergeant Major,
Crack! went the sound of our tender bones shattering,
Rip! went the sound of our flesh-blistering skin.
But still, on we fought; with half empty hope, of recognition.

With a fatal blow to his head, my friend fell before me,
Soon after we were overcome by tedious murky gas.
As we searched frantically for our gas masks,
Companions were dropping down, choking like chickens,
Fighting for clean, fresh air.
Helplessly I stood there astounded, pleading survival for my friends.
Reluctantly, we carried on, people who were once my best friends,
now just deceased limp bodies, waiting to be picked up and discarded
like pieces of rubbish.

Soon it would be nightfall and the sullen grounds would once again
fall silent,
As in the cryptic night we would lie awake, licking our wounds
and wallowing in pity.
You may call it bravery, but in our eyes it's menacing, precarious
and immoral.

At last we fall asleep, with weak limbs and bad nightmares,
penetrating the body.
We fight not only for justice, but to demolish the lives of innocent ones,
But although it's wrong, I *will* have courage and I *will* fight
for my country.

Laura Atkinson (14)
Bideford College, Bideford

The Thing That Shocked The Girl

There was a girl who woke up,
The room she was in was dark,
She sat up and listened intently,
While she did this she heard a bark.

She sat up and listened intently,
While biting her blood-red nail,
Wondering who was out there,
She looked so fragile and pale.

Wondering who was out there,
She crawled out of the big soft bed,
She crept along the landing,
When she looked she saw a moving head.

She crept along the landing,
She saw the whole figure,
She wondered who this strange person was,
So she pulled the bloody trigger.

She wondered who this strange person was,
She flicked on the light to get a better view,
She stepped down the stairs,
To her surprise it was someone she knew!

She stepped down the stairs,
To her horror the bloodstained mirror was shattered at her feet.
She dropped the gun she held to the ground,
She stepped back with blood dripping from her heart as it
                        took its final beat.

Clare Penny (14)
Bideford College, Bideford

Racism

The other week
A friend of mine
Took a bullet in the back
There wasn't any particular reason
It was just because he is black.

I have to be careful
Where I walk
And even where I eat
Because you never know
What's going to happen
When you're walking down the street.

I don't understand
Why people have a problem
With my religion
Or my race
Because the only thing that separates us,
Is the colour of my face.

Now all I ask
Is that I can
Live a normal life just like you
But with all these people
Out to get me
I find that hard to do.

So please if you see me
Don't be so quick off the mark
To shout abuse at me
Just because my skin is dark.

Emma Wilson (14)
Bideford College, Bideford

Be Who You Are!

Stand tall and proud,
Do not slouch and hide,
Make an impression,
Show some pride.

If people laugh and stare,
Bury the feeling deep,
Just ignore those faces,
Take that massive leap.

Don't just stand there,
Waiting to be found,
Don't be pushed about,
Find your solid ground.

If people trip you up
And snigger at what you wear,
Don't give 'em satisfaction
Of showing that you care.

Try to drown that sinking feeling,
Gripping at your heart,
But you and your real self,
Should never be apart.

They laugh at your bad work,
As you blush and cry with shame,
All the things that people say,
Make you feel you're not the same.

All these people around you
Make you remember the things that you lack,
So waste no time, stand up proud
And answer them right back!

Leah Jeffery (14)
Bideford College, Bideford

Running Free

I think sometimes on what it's like to be,
A sheep, pig, goat or fish in the sea.

To be trapped in a tank all alone
Or to be won at a fair and shoved in a bag
Squashed with no space and clipped with a tag.

Foxes running for their life
Behind them are men on horses and dogs that are vicious and tough
20 dogs behind him, he surely won't live, they're all so big and rough.

Monkeys being dressed up at a circus and used for entertainment
Everyone says it's really funny, so people want to see
While the monkey wants to run to his home and be with his family.

Stuck in a tank,
Being hunted down,
Using their fur to make a gown,
We should treat animals as we'd like to be,
So open the cages and let them free.

Ruby Hudson
Bideford College, Bideford

Newcastle

The harbour
Once the marvel of Newcastle
Now a dwindling yard
The cranes were once all over
Now there's only 1 or 2.

The cranes
Once constantly in motion
Now an inch or two a day
They must be so lonely
Standing there all day.

Adam Bowman (14)
Carmel Technology College, Darlington

Jaws

Sharks are grey just like your aunt May,
They will take your leg away
And they will not stop and stay.
Jaws ate a boy on a lilo,
It must have reminded him of Dido.
The man in the red boat had
No chance to float,
He did not give a goat
When his leg began to float.
Jaws' skin is silky,
It makes his victims taste milky.
He is very vicious,
And even more malicious.

Liam Coates (14)
Carmel Technology College, Darlington

Sunset

Dark
Black skies
Waiting for a moon
Looking for stars.
Cold
Burnt fires
Flames have gone
Glowing cinders failing.
Quiet
Empty streets
No one is walking
Sparkle
Bright halo
End of a rainbow
Glowing colourful clouds.

Charlotte McAuley (14)
Carmel Technology College, Darlington

Make Poverty History

Children dying, ill and hungry
No water, no food and lack of money.

On the streets they shall lie
Waiting and waiting but then they die.

Living rough, no shelter to sleep
In an alley with children to keep.

Piercing screams from a baby in pain
No drinks or snacks, not a drop of rain.

Buying a white band only costs a pound
With that, imagine how that baby could sound.

We need to stop this here and now
Or another human being will just pass out.

This shouldn't happen, not anywhere
But does their government even care?

Gabrielle McKenna (13)
Carmel Technology College, Darlington

My Annoying Little Brother

My annoying little brother always gets me into trouble,
He goes crying to my mum and makes my blood bubble.

My annoying little brother is always in the wrong,
He gets on my nerves, I wish I could send him to Hong Kong.

If I'm on the trampoline he has to be on too,
I want to be by myself, why doesn't he get the clue?

My annoying little brother copies everything I say.
I like night-time when he's not there, but then there's the next day.

Emma Galbraith (12)
Carmel Technology College, Darlington

Rugby Is The Game

Rugby is the game
Newcastle Falcons are the fame,
While the crowd eat the pies,
The players get the tries.

Wilkinson converts
And Shaw reverts
The crowd stand tall
While the players get ready for the mall.

The game is coming to an end
The players defend
The crowd jump from the rows
The final whistle blows.

Rugby is the game.

Liam Campbell (13)
Carmel Technology College, Darlington

Summer!

On a lovely hot summer's day,
In the middle of May,
There was a bright hot sun,
With plenty of children having fun,
While all the women lay on their towels,
All the men are shouting, 'Foul',
Because they are playing football,
But they are not that tall,
So as you can see,
There are no bees,
But soon they will go back home,
Back to their homes,
Then back to bed,
Without being fed.

Amy Raper (12)
Carmel Technology College, Darlington

Yellow Spotted Lizard

Y ellow eyes as bright as the sun
E xactly 11 yellow spots on them
L iving in the shade, afraid of the sun
I ying down all day, nothing to do
O ut of the shade their skin crackles and burns
W himpering and whining because there's no shade.

S cales so bright you're blind
P eople are scared and run away
O nions are the things that keep them away
T rees are good shade, but there are none
T riumphant victories of killing victims
E very drop of blood gone
D ead people now there are.

L apping up blood from unlucky passers-by
I nside holes it's nice and cool
Z ebras are not in the lizards' way
A gain another passer dies
R ed flaps of skin over yellow eyes
D emon lizards are here now.

Sean Kelly (13)
Carmel Technology College, Darlington

Winter

Cold condensed windows bleed with icy breath
Sharp raw snow wanders with the frozen wind
Solitary winds pierce vulnerable skin, maliciously probing
Winter appears to alienate nature, but life still goes on.

James Smith (13)
Carmel Technology College, Darlington

The Widow

The widow that walks
That lonely stretch
Of vast, unwanted moorland
Looks up to the sky
And sighs a soft sigh
Wondering when she shall join him,
Why, oh why
Did he leave so soon
Leaving her in this new, scary, modern world?

Well, she is not sad,
She is too
Mad to even think about food,
Left on her own
Nobody at all to talk to,
He took his life for no reason
The questions linger in the air
People searching for the answer,
But some things they'll never know.

Stephanie Spence (13)
Carmel Technology College, Darlington

Hobbies

H opping over hurdles is what I like to do
O bstacles are no problem, I can do them too
B adminton I enjoy, hitting shuttlecocks all day
B owling the skittles down is a game I like to play
I ce skating without falling over is the aim
E mma is my name and sport is my game
S wimming is the best, but I do like all the rest!

Emma Hird (13)
Carmel Technology College, Darlington

The Tiger

Beneath the canopy of the rainforest,
A creature prowling, that is blessed
With fur the colour of blazing fire,
And streaks of black, forbidding and dire.

Its teeth like daggers, designed to bite,
Its roar fills all who hear it with fright,
The silent stalk, the sudden kill,
Then stops to feed, and eats its fill.

But now it's on the endangered list,
The poacher against the naturalist,
For possessed of such a splendid hide,
Vain human owners are filled with pride.

However, all is not lost for this spectacular creature,
For throughout the rainforest, there is a new feature,
Safe havens for such an endangered beast,
So it's still seen prowling throughout the east.

Jonathan Lumsdon (13)
Carmel Technology College, Darlington

The Summer Sun

Amidst its rise and fall
The red star shines brightly
Its heat liberates men from cold,
Its rays warm the ground gently.

Amidst its giving of life,
The sleeping mammals awaken,
The grassy meadows, so green,
The sun's present given.

Amidst the lengthening days,
The sun lights up the previous night.
Luxurious evenings of sunlit sky,
Summer in all its might.

Dillon Zhou (12)
Carmel Technology College, Darlington

Jack The Ripper

In dark and dreary London town
There is a man upon whom everyone does frown.
This villainous man is a child of the night,
But he could be anyone at day's first light.
Through dark London streets he goes,
Who he is, no one knows!
Cutting, slashing, tearing, ripping!

Following him about is death,
He watches his victim's last breath.
Steps in a large pool of blood,
Then walks outside in the mud.
He'll enter your house when you're in bed
Once he's been in you'll end up dead!
Cutting, slashing, tearing, ripping!

He is the demon of London town,
When he is near you, you'll fall down.
The midnight bell begins to chime,
Killing is his favourite pastime.
Quick, ring a bell!
He is a demon from Hell!
Cutting, slashing, tearing, ripping!

Elizabeth Sutcliffe (14)
Carmel Technology College, Darlington

The Old Woman In The Sun

As green as the grass,
The trees that grow,
As I can see through
This small window.

Not a cloud in the sky,
So clear and bright,
As I can see through
This small window.

The children are
Playing, singing and dancing,
As I can see through
This small window.

The birds are singing,
So high in tune,
As I can see through
This small window.

I sit here day after day,
I see everything passing my way,
Through this small window.

Lewis Brown (12)
Carmel Technology College, Darlington

River Tyne

The ships that once sailed by are now just a memory
Now there's nothing on the Tyne
There's a part of Newcastle left back in time.
The big river was long ago
But no one really wants to know.
No more ships on the river
But good old Newcastle is still a giver.
The ships left one by one
As if they'd been scared off by a bomb.
The river flows gently
It's lost its life
Just like a man without his wife.
The only hopes the Tyne's got is its nightlife
It's got a lot!
From birthdays to hen nights, it's got them all
Believe me, Newcastle isn't small.

Gavin Rodgers (14)
Carmel Technology College, Darlington

Holidays

The sun twinkles upon the sea
The waves lap on the shore with glee.

The sun beams onto your neck
You won't get burnt, I don't suspect.

Take a paddle in the sea
Then let's all go home for tea.

Sitting in the lounge drinking wine
Holidays in the summertime.

It's time to go to bed
You've got a sore head.

Wake up bright and early
Your hair is now curly!

Philip Massingham (12)
Carmel Technology College, Darlington

Geordie Land

Haweh lads, let's gan doon toon,
Not every night, it's Fridays awnly,
Pull a lass in the loud crowd
Get some Brown Ale down my neck.

Ower the bridge and far away,
Alan Shearer comes to play
Skins, shoots, scores, one-nil
The crowd gans wild.

Cars and buses everywhere
Watched over by the Angel of the North
People pass the massive angel,
Maybe really far from home.

Great North Run every year
There's a pub somewhere near
Gan'n round the Millennium Bridge
Get in soon, beer in the fridge.

(Home at last!)

Andrew James Clifford (13)
Carmel Technology College, Darlington

Geordie Culture

Across the bridge the shimmering Tyne
And on the left St James' Park
Where people from all over come and see
Their heroes play
Well what a sight on a cold winter's day.

Inside the ground the cheering fans
As Newcastle score 1-0
Then a sigh of relief as the match is over
As Newcastle win again.
Then down to the pub for Brown Ale.

Jessica Wake (13)
Carmel Technology College, Darlington

Jaws

The busy beaches underneath the sunny skies,
Nobody there is very wise.
Anything could be in the sea,
Something that could attack you and me.

Children splashing on yellow rings,
Making sandcastles, a little boy sings.
Under the water something is there,
Is anybody there aware?

It's swimming under and all around,
It isn't making a sound.
Up it jumps to everyone's surprise,
Nobody knew it was there for they weren't wise.

It grabs a boy with its big white teeth,
And grabs him down to the coral reef.
Rips and shreds at his body parts,
Hands, eyes, liver and heart.

People rushing out the water,
Running away from hideous slaughter.
His mother has just realised,
You can see the fear in her eyes.

Rachel Musgrave (13)
Carmel Technology College, Darlington

Jaws Attack

You see it lurking,
In the lagoon.
You know it's coming,
By the eerie tune.

You can't see it round you,
You can only see the lagoon floor,
You then feel its jagged teeth
That feels just like a saw.

The sea so blue, so very empty,
Everyone has fled.
Then the water changes rapidly,
To a bright, blood-red!

You know that you won't survive,
As it keeps on biting
But you know you shouldn't give in,
So then you keep on fighting.

The shark then starts to win,
Its bites feel like darts
Then it takes you away
As it rips you apart.

Thomas Haile (14)
Carmel Technology College, Darlington

My Culture Poem

Newcastle is the place to be,
Friday night drinks on me.

There are so many different places to go and see,
That big eye and Tyne, there's so many places you could be.

The football stadium is full of fans,
Having a laugh with a few cans.

Go and see who is doing the Great North Run
It's a load of fun!

Go and shop at the Eldon Square
So many things to see and wear.

Finish your day with a nice drink,
Anything other than ale goes down the sink.

Hannah Pritchard (13)
Carmel Technology College, Darlington

Speed Of The Night

Drivers all ready, get on the line
Adrenaline rushing, waiting for the sign
Engines are revving, the prize is in sight
Wheels start spinning, there's the green light.

Blazing through the streets, powerslides and all
One racer is out, their Impreza has hit a wall
Three cars left, pedestrians running away
Police cars start chasing, 'Floor it!' they all say.

Outrunning the cops, nitro at the ready
Cars blasting forward, struggling to keep them steady
Another car crashes, it's totally wrecked
Only two left, it's what you would expect.

Side by side, neck and neck
A car is in the way, quick, hit the deck
One driver swerves and misses the cars
The other driver crashes, the winner gets 1,000 dollars.

Kieren Kemp (14)
Carmel Technology College, Darlington

This Truly Is The City Of Geordies

The Tyne river winds through this city,
Down and round the Newcastle crowd,
Whispering sounds of the history found,
Of the ship-building harbour that is renowned.

Visions of flatcaps and hands of beer,
Men that are hard not to hear,
Busy buildings loaded with sales,
People laden with heavy shopping bags.

Nightclubs illuminate the city and out come
The short skirts and lads,
Everyone going out for a treat,
Then on the way home
They're dizzy in the streets.
This truly is the city where Geordies live
And tell their tale.

Emma Bantleman (14)
Carmel Technology College, Darlington

Two Thousand Years

Two thousand years of voices echo,
Along dark alleys and churches old,
Down ancient roads a thousand memories
Go like unseen ghosts in a world of age and mystery.
The silent funnels like looming giants
Cast dark shadows over this sleeping city.
The castle's high walls far above echo
Of long won battles, past hopes and dreams.
The crest of Newcastle is as old as mystery itself.
Though this is no relic or ruined city,
And above the darkness of old city remains
A new, bright and vibrant city glitters through the dark.

Patrick Wharton (14)
Carmel Technology College, Darlington

Geordie Culture

The rising sun glints off the giant Millennium Bridge
Reflecting the warm shades of yellow,
The sleeping city rests below,
Basking in the silent, superior image.

Cars begin to purr and sirens wail like cats,
Dim street lights fade as the day jumps to a stare,
Children kick up pigeons, screaming as they quack,
And adults slump to work, with a sinking heart.

As one o'clock chimes,
The workers pause, to have a filling lunch
Steak pie and greasy chip time,
They're dying for a munch.

When the time comes, the children flee home,
After a tiring day of play,
Six o'clock passes and on the streets no one roams
Teatime's the best time of day.

The deep blue evening falls, but this city does not stop,
Bouncing beats and laughter fill the air,
The bars are overflowing and in the clubs people bop,
Dancing and drinking till the early hours flare.

When the nightclubs are all drained and the drunks return home,
Deep darkness rests like a heavy velvet sheet,
The city revisits its hushed tone,
Until the sun and sky again meet.

Jessica Conway (14)
Carmel Technology College, Darlington

Newcastle

In Newcastle city centre flows the rapid River Tyne,
Over it sits the gateway between your city and mine,
With its modern structure and incredible archway,
The bustle of city life passes over it every day.

Newcastle United - haway the lads!
The fans all love 'em, sons and dads.
With Alan Shearer running down the pitch
Crowds turn out in their thousands, making him rich.

For fabulous fashion, the Metro's the word
And for delux designers there's Eldon Square, I've heard.
As hundreds of shoppers flash their cash every day,
It's a wonder they've still got money to pay!

Then there's Baltic Flour Mill,
Contemporary art, what a thrill!
With ten thousand square metres of space,
Hurry along, reserve your place!

Stop by for a traditional teatime,
To not try the steak and kidney pie would be a crime,
Or go to the pub, sample the legendary Newcastle Brown Ale,
With the place full of men, there's plenty for sale.

Dancing, cheering, rows and fights,
Just another of Newcastle's Friday nights,
From pub to club the people move,
Until they settle down and find their groove.

The Angel of the North greets all who enter,
Welcoming them to the gorgeous city centre,
With so much to do and lots of sights to see,
Newcastle's a great place for you and for me!

Rebecca Eldrington (14)
Carmel Technology College, Darlington

Geordie

Geordies' life is far from normal,
Their attitude seems somewhat informal.

The Geordies are a friendly race,
Newcastle is a party place.

They speak in a funny way,
Can't understand a word they say.

The Angel of the North stands tall,
This city welcomes one and all.

Famous for the Great North Run,
Thousands come for this day of fun.

The River Tyne was used to carry coal,
Now it is the city's soul.

Many bridges cross the mighty Tyne,
Upon this town the sun does shine.

Newcastle Brown Ale is their choice of drink,
While their wives work at the kitchen sink.

Black 'n' white's the colour of their team,
At St James' Park the crowds do scream.

The Metro Centre provides fantastic shopping,
Once they start - there is no stopping.

With thousands of designers galore,
They need money for evermore.

Lindisfarne, Alan Shearer and Andy Capp
Have all helped put this place on the map.

Katie Oxley (14)
Carmel Technology College, Darlington

Geordie Culture

Women at home,
Working all day,
Men at the pub,
Drinking their pay.

A well-known chav,
Called Andy Capp,
Helps put that toon,
Onto the map.

The Blayden Races
St James' Park
All the nightlife,
After dark.

All those shops
Too many to choose,
Newcastle match,
They're bound to lose!

Their favourite pie,
The steak and kidney,
The new glass Sage,
A bit like in Sydney.

The Millennium Bridge,
Built over the Tyne,
Built in 2000,
It's a great design.

Well I hope you've learnt more,
About this toon,
You'd have a great time,
So come visit soon!

Sophie Mackay (14)
Carmel Technology College, Darlington

Life On The Tyne

Tyne, Tyne, go back in time,
To the years of industry that had begun,
With deep coal mines,
And progressive ship building,
That was a strength of a north eastern man.
The big steel ships, with their engines roaring,
Sailing their way through that busy river,
And the bridges in front of their path
Stood tall with its arms stretched out wide,
Gripping the land, as it was proud of itself,
Knowing it's part of the north east workforce.
Alongside the river, lined, steep, smog-ridden
Streets with their crammed town housing and backyard laundry.
Here live the Geordie people,
Who live their life to the full
With their strong northern accent
Which stand above all the rest
And all that singing, dancing, drinking and spending,
Loads of their money,
Still having so much fun,
I wonder how they had time to invent the
North East Run?

Adam Bell (14)
Carmel Technology College, Darlington

Summer

Sitting having fun,
Under a blaze of sun.

The heat of the sun is so hot,
People eating ice lollies a lot.

Looking up at the sky
Watching the fluffy clouds
Go by.

Sadie McCartney (13)
Carmel Technology College, Darlington

Geordie Culture

The streets are as black as the night,
You can see shadows creeping around you,
Wherever you look,
The bridge dominates the skyline,
You can see the shadows casting over the city,
A dark and dangerous creature ready to catch its prey.
The Sage brings entertainment to the north,
It brings all different cultures, ages and music together.
The food is carefully home-made
It brings people together,
And shows their culture,
The Newcastle Brown Ale is famous,
So many have tasted it,
They say it's beautifully smooth,
They have a language
That brings them together,
'Are you for real or what?'
The ship industry looms over them,
The ships used to glide smoothly down the Tyne,
Now that's all in the past,
It's been put to rest,
The nightlife gives the people of
Newcastle time to shine like stars.

Sinead Wisker (14)
Carmel Technology College, Darlington

Summer Holidays

The summer holidays are so fun,
Sitting all day and playing in the sun.
Me and Emma having a water fight,
Playing all through the day and night.
Eating ice cream all day long,
Sunbathing and thinking what I've done wrong.
As the sun makes me red,
I am so tired now I want my bed.

Laura Myers (12)
Carmel Technology College, Darlington

Geordie Culture

The bridge stands as tall as the eye can see
As it stretches its arms over an open Tyne
People cross over this quiet, calming sea
To seek their education or go out to dine.

The houses are terraced, simple and small
They are nothing special just a little bit stale
Industries working away providing jobs for all
While others go to the pub and get hammered with ale.

The nightlife is quiet, as quiet as stars,
While people come back from a hard day of work
On their way home they might stop at a café or bar
Have a pint or a nice cup of char.

One by one street lights go out as dawn on Tyneside breaks
A Geordie falls out of bed and groans himself awake
His wife moans, 'I'm sick of the hangovers.'
He swears as he's done each day
This week, 'Tonight I will be sober.'

William Jones (14)
Carmel Technology College, Darlington

Food!

It's here, there and everywhere,
From a lobster to a juicy pear!
The famous Indian dish is curry,
But at McDonald's you get a McFlurry.
From the Chinese I get beef satay,
Have a nice coffee, mmmm . . . latte!
Spain, famous for its paella,
But the English go mad for Nutella!
Ya can't beat a good old roast,
For breakie, it's jam on toast.
Well that's food
And yes it's true
No one loves it as much as you!

Abbi Fluen (14)
Carmel Technology College, Darlington

Upon Tyne

A dominating bridge guards the river
North-blowing winds to make you shiver
Packed houses with cobbled streets
Ships, one waiting to be complete.

Now the river is no longer the city's centre
An angel greets all who enter
History's lost with the passing of time
History that was yours and mine.

From the ancestors of old
To our generation so bold
Newcastle upon Tyne
S'all mine, all mine.

Victoria McAfee (15)
Carmel Technology College, Darlington

Geordie Culture

St James's Park
What a place to be
Everyone's rocking off their tree
As if they got in for free.

The iron bridge that's on the Tyne
What a piece of art, that's fine
Oh, I wish it was mine
Then I could afford to dine.

The 'Angel' stands very tall
Let's make sure it doesn't fall
It is the gateway to the massive hall
It is definitely not small.

With mining being their way of life
Ship building and tourism now sees more life
With the Tyne carrying the many memories.

Daryl King (14)
Carmel Technology College, Darlington

Ocean

Amongst the deep blue sea,
Beware of the dangers there is to be.
Fish swimming here and there,
Looking out for evil everywhere.

Treasure hidden underneath the coral,
Waiting for someone to quarrel.
Look, a man has spotted his prize,
But really he should have opened his eyes.

Lurking around is the mouth of death,
He may never have a fresh new breath.
For behind him is a gigantic shark,
Which he did not see in the dark.

Lucky as he was,
He will probably be here tomorrow because,
The treasure filled him with temptation,
So all for nothing was his salvation.

Alisha Sinha (14)
Carmel Technology College, Darlington

Music

Music is a way of life
Listen to the sound
It's much better than having a wife
Jumping on the ground.
In your house
On the stage
Read the music
Page by page
If you hate the music life
You might as well go and find a wife.

Christopher Thomas Ward (13)
Carmel Technology College, Darlington

Geordie Culture

Newcastle is cool with lots of lights
Men and women are wearing tights,
Newcastle Brown Ale is very fizzy
So much it is, it makes you dizzy.

All of Newcastle follows their sport
They like it so much they might go to court,
They get into fights with all different regions
We do not know why they do this, there are no reasons.

After all this place is nice
It is so clean with not any lice,
They love their city
And because they do they make it pretty.

They have landmarks that are very good
They are upon grass and lots of mud,
This place is a good one that is so great
This place never sleeps until very late.

Ross Kelly (14)
Carmel Technology College, Darlington

Lunchtime

12 o'clock Friday, lunch has begun,
Time for a world of games and fun.

The lads come out one by one
Eating crisps and chewing gum.

The match begins with a laugh
The lads are really acting daft.

I'm in goal, Clifford's defending
We score a goal, the match is ending.

Lunch is over,
This is what I'm dreading!

Luke Williamson (14)
Carmel Technology College, Darlington

Splendid Seaside

Splendid seaside is the best,
Why don't you come and take off your vest,
And go in the crystal-blue sea,
That looks as clear as glass.

Children have their buckets and spades,
Ready to go and make some sandcastles,
While their mums and dads sit in the shade,
Reading their magazines.

Other children in their costumes,
Ready to go and play in the sea,
They haven't got long,
Before they have to go home for their tea.

When the clouds are moving towards them,
Parents shout to their children to watch out,
As it looks like it is going to rain,
And the tide is coming further in.

The wind picks up
Making waves clash on rocks
Children run to their parents
As they are unsafe next to the sea.

As the day comes to an end
All of the children say
That was one splendid day!

Stephanie Metcalfe (13)
Carmel Technology College, Darlington

Summertime

Sweat is dripping
From the end of my nose
My fingers are boiling
And so are my toes.

As all the birds glide
In the lovely blue sky
We build a sandcastle
As the time flies.

All the exams
Are a week away
We're going through
The hottest day.

The sun's like gold
Shining in the sky
Then an ice cream van
Caught my eye.

The grass is nice, fine, green
And the plants are quite appealing
But if I sniff a dandelion
That would be deceiving.

When I get home
I'll have a water fight with mates
Till the sun goes down
Which will be quite late.

Ben Foster (12)
Carmel Technology College, Darlington

The Charge Of The Redcoats

The drums are beating
The flags are flying
The soldiers are marching on
The ground just rumbles, rumbles, rumbles
The cannons fire ceaselessly on
The ground just rumbles, rumbles, rumbles
The voices in soldiers' simple minds tell them to run away
But the heroic part of their simple minds
Tells them to fight and stay.
When the two lines stop and present their guns,
All the soldiers in the first two lines think, 'Oh, crumbs!'
Musket fire rips into the ranks and kills so many souls.
The gold cross belt of the elite French are stained with red, not gold
The redcoats shout their fearsome chants
And brandish their big, long swords
Swinging them high and then they descend
On their small prey and so many of them will die.
The battle was fierce, but victory came to the British
So there ends the charge of the redcoats.

Richard McAllister (13)
Carmel Technology College, Darlington

The Summer Beach

The blazing gold grains of sand run through people's toes
The huge waves crash against people's beetroot burnt skin.
People screaming and laughing like there was a pantomime on show.
Then it ceased.
Freezing blue drops fell from the murky clouds
The waves became fierce and a storm was approaching.
People running, people shouting, people leaving the
                               bitter cold beach for good.

Rebecca King (12)
Carmel Technology College, Darlington

Billy And The Bin

It would all begin by putting Billy in the bin,
We were going to play a game, but because Billy is so lame,
He sat right in the way, where we were going to play,
The sun was hot, our brains were going to rot.
Not only is Billy lazy, but he started going crazy, so
We asked him to move, but he just said, 'No.'
What would we have to prove to get him to go.
It was getting late, no longer we could wait,
So Josh picked him up as though he was a young pup
And threw him in a tin that is known as a bin
But Billy would not take and threw Josh in the lake
So Billy our friend no more, now he knows the score,
And so it all began by putting Billy in the bin.

Andrew Jordan (13)
Carmel Technology College, Darlington

The World We Live In

Everywhere around us people are dying,
Friends and family everyone's crying.
Bombs are going off in different places,
Each and everyday we see new faces.

Psychos and murderers running around,
People just trying to keep their feet on the ground.
This world is black and hearts are cold,
There's no hope that's what we're told.

Some take the easy way out and slip away,
Innocent people died without their say.
But others hold on and pray for the best
This world we live in should have a rest.

Abby Clarke (13)
Carmel Technology College, Darlington

Holiday

The sandy beaches
And lushing waves
No more school
It's just great.

The palm trees
Swaying in the breeze
I'm red like a tomato
And hot like the sun.

The fun has just begun
Swimming and diving
Laughing and playing
Sunbathing.

Long sunny days
Is just what I like
No exams, no sports day
Just relaxing all day long.

Rachel Baines (12)
Carmel Technology College, Darlington

Summer Holidays

The steamy air is hot,
The ice cold drinks are not,
There is a very pig pod,
Far, far away from school,
Adults are not at work,
All children have no homework,
Everyone's relaxed,
On holiday, on holiday.

Nicola Bleasby (13)
Carmel Technology College, Darlington

Bad Summer Holidays

As summer comes so do the dreadful holidays
The airports swarming with people
The aeroplanes are all delayed
The waiting area at sweltering temperatures.

As summer comes so do the horrible holidays
Airless buses travelling to hotels,
Hotel rooms, minute like ants
Beds squeaking like mice.

As summer comes so do the terrible holidays
Children shrieking by the pool
The water packed with red, scorched people
Dead insects drifting on the surface.

As summer comes so do the awful holidays
Everything goes wrong
So much commotion, is it worth it
Just for a trip to Birmingham?

Paul McDermott (12)
Carmel Technology College, Darlington

School Trip

Off we went on our trip
Sat on the coach with two hours to go
What can we do, does anyone know?
We sit and talk and do our hair
Oh, how long is left until we get there?
We see the signs only 10 miles away
So not long to go, hip hip hooray!
We get off the coach and it's pouring with rain
Oh, now I want to go back home again!

Sarah McDonogh (15)
Carmel Technology College, Darlington

What The Geordies Do!

The sun rises in Newcastle
Early in the morning
It reflects on the River Tyne
Setting the water on fire.

Geordies gather in the streets,
Ready to see the Magpies fly around the pitch
They drink their Brown Ale in St James' Park,
As the stadium lights glisten in the dark.

As the nightlife staggers across the Millennium Bridge,
The river snakes underneath it.
The street lights dance on the ripples of the water,
As the horizon finally meets it.

As the Geordies walk home from St James' Park,
And the nightlife from the bars
Everything becomes silent and still,
Until next time!

Stacey Marie Clegg (14)
Carmel Technology College, Darlington

Looking Back

Looking forward, looking back,
So many things to lose,
Wishing we could turn back time
So that you didn't blow that fuse.

When you left, my whole world stopped,
No minutes, hours or seconds changed,
I lived in a world that was constantly locked
With no one but me to be saved.

Rachael Peeke (14)
Carmel Technology College, Darlington

On Your Marks, Get Set, Go!

They're off, Jack is in the first lane, running very fast,
Nile is in the second, full of life
But where is Sam?

Sam is sat in the cold, dull and boring exam hall,
He is sat watching the clock waiting for the test to finish.

Meanwhile Nile is winning the race,
But Jack is rapidly running and he is catching up,
In the blazing and the heart-stopping race no one knows who will win.

The test is almost over,
Sam is answering the last question.
The hall is empty,
Everyone is watching the big race.

As they come into the home straight,
It is neck and neck,
They are passing the shouting and colourful crowd,
But Jack has tripped over,
Nile takes the winner's medal!

Neil Hanlon (12)
Carmel Technology College, Darlington

Make Poverty History

Every 3 seconds a child dies
Every 3 seconds a mother cries
Every 3 seconds while I stuff my face
A malnourished African waits for aid
Every 3 seconds we campaign, end the hunger and the pain
Every 3 seconds we plead, end the suffering,
Make poverty history.

Jack Meredith (15)
Carmel Technology College, Darlington

Questions

What is it about you
That means I can't let go?
All the bad you came to do
Yet my heart still won't say *no!*

So how do you manage to control,
My life without being around?
Your cold hands grasp my soul
And in misery I begin to drown.

Why is it that you destroyed me,
My mind, soul and heart?
I guess it was never meant to be,
As now we are living two worlds apart.

My life is filled with so many complications
Twists, turns and so many roads to take
So how could I compete with your life's simplifications?
As you live in a world where there's no need to fake.

Kyrie J Hunter (15)
Carmel Technology College, Darlington

The Wind

The wind was howling and blowing through the trees
The rain bounced off the road and gushed down the drains
Like a fast flowing river
The sky grew darker and darker
As the black thunder clouds took over the sky
The thunder became louder as it drew closer.
The lightning was bright and lit up the sky
Huge bolts came down bouncing off the ground.

Kathryn Hall (15)
Carmel Technology College, Darlington

Football Crazy

The crowds gather outside the stadium like cattle
Preparing like Vikings to go into battle.
Once inside the ginormous place
The two teams come face to face
A player goes and takes a dive
Now we see the teams collide.
Fans start shouting and waving their arms
The referee tries to keep everyone calm
A penalty is given, the fans start to scream
The other team hope it wasn't seen.
The captain steps up and kicks the ball
It smacks the back of the net as the goalie falls.
One-nil, full-time both teams are battered
Fans want to go to sleep as they're completely shattered
They leave losers and don't know the reason.
To win the cup again they'll have to wait till next season.

Jonathan Way (15)
Carmel Technology College, Darlington

King Of The Hills

Avalanche soared
Over the rolling hills,
He flew like the wind
Ready to kill.

Avalanche dived,
With a glint in his eyes,
The mouse he caught,
Gave a pitiful cry.

Avalanche the owl,
Looked satisfied
The king of the hills
Was full of pride.

Natasha Redpath (13)
Carmel Technology College, Darlington

Summertime

Summer, summer
Really fun
Bees, bees
Better run.

Burns, burns
Really hurt,
Boys, boys,
Better flirt.

Lollies, lollies
Really nice,
Orange, blackcurrant,
Solid ice.

Summer, summer
Now it has gone,
Cold, cold
The sun has shone.

Emma Spraggon (12)
Carmel Technology College, Darlington

The Army

The army is a tough place,
Where you have to complete the obstacle course in a fast pace.
Aiming the rifle at your enemy
Deciding to attack or to flee.
Crouching down, keeping my cool,
Deciding not to move, making myself a fool.
Looking back calling for help,
The shining bullet hits me, I let out a yelp.

Christopher Clinton (15)
Carmel Technology College, Darlington

Summer Sun, Hot Days

Summer sun, hot days
Over 100 Fahrenheit!
Having fun all day long
Even at 10pm it's bright.

Summer sun, hot days
Is the heat here to stay?
The cool breeze is always welcome,
All the time, every day.

Summer sun, hot days,
Bathing by the deep blue sea.
Looking at the horizon,
As far away as can be.

Summer sun, hot days,
Sun is undoubtedly in the sky.
The sauntering heat is unbearable
As on this golden beach I lie.

Michael Thurloway (13)
Carmel Technology College, Darlington

Missing You

Little guardian angel,
Little ray of light
Lift me up when I feel down
Protect me through the night.

Skipping up and down the grass,
I saw you every day.
I never wanted days to pass,
All I wanted was to play.

You haven't really gone at all,
You'll always be with me.
I talk to you, I pray, I call
My love, my angel be.

Christina Muller (13)
Carmel Technology College, Darlington

Summertime

In the summer sun
My creativity really starts to come.

Sports in the summer sun
Can get a bit overwhelming
But exciting like sports day.

The long days can make you very
Exhausted and very, very hot.

When I think of summer
I think of my birthday
And the six week holidays.

The beaches with all that
Hot sand and cool sea water.

Bethany Harper (12)
Carmel Technology College, Darlington

Summer Garden

I walk down my garden
Through the summer air,
I see the beautiful plants
My fingertips touch their velvet petals
They're as dry as bones,
I water them,
To bring them back to life,
The sparkling water gleams,
My mum lies there relaxed and burning bright red.
I see glistening water shoot through the air,
I realise it's my brother splashing everywhere.
I lay there in silence
In the sun's hot rays
What a wonderful time in the garden,
I spend every day there.

Louise Sowerby (12)
Carmel Technology College, Darlington

Summertime

As the sun comes out
And begins to shine,
Everyone is glad,
Now it's summertime!

At school it's sports day
We're having loads of fun,
The athletes are sweating,
Under the beating sun.

Now it's exams,
We're sitting in the hall,
This is so boring,
Staring at the wall.

It's the end of school,
Everyone's going away
Off to a foreign place,
For their summer holidays.

Then we're back at school,
The weather's just rain,
Sitting in the classroom,
Waiting for summer again.

Thomas Wilson (12)
Carmel Technology College, Darlington

Sports Day

The crowds gathering to the field
Chatting, shouting mouths they wield
To cheer their athlete on.

The stands are filling to the seams
And every person in their dreams
Hopes their athlete wins.

The athletes are emerging from school
Through the massive, shouting pool
Of people cheering them on.

The athletes are shaking and vibrating
And wondering whether they will be king
Of the race they will compete in.

On your marks! They crouch down to the ground
Set! There is silence, nothing making sound
Muscles tensing, people anxious then . . .
Go!

James Potts (11)
Carmel Technology College, Darlington

Football

'F oul,' they cried,
'O ffside,' shouted the referee,
O utrage was felt by the crowd
T en-nil to Rangers
B ellamy has been injured (ha, ha)
A t Ranger's stadium all are happy
L iars are Celtic
L oudmouths too!

Hollie McLean (11)
Eastbourne Secondary School, Darlington

Poverty

P is for poverty and people who are hungry
O is to observe the people who have nothing
V is for vision to have a dream
E is for everything but having everything is nothing
R is for rights that they do not have
T is for tired, tired for searching for food.
Y is for you, why don't you help?

Declan Franklin (13)
Eastbourne Secondary School, Darlington

Fairies

Fairies at the bottom of my garden
Fairies dancing, singing at the bottom of my garden
They jump up and down at the bottom of my garden
They play hide-and-seek at the bottom of my garden
I love playing at the bottom of my garden.

Jennifer Hinde (12)
Eastbourne Secondary School, Darlington

Money

M any things to buy
O nly need so much
N ow and then to spend it
E veryone wants to smell it
Y oung and old, we love it.

Simon Kieran (13)
Eastbourne Secondary School, Darlington

The Night

The night
Dark
Scary
Stars glaring at you

The moon
The moon is full
The stars are staring at you

Stranger, stranger
Who are you?
You're scary
I am looking at you.

Declan Gregory (12)
Eastbourne Secondary School, Darlington

Parents! Parents!

Parents never believe a thing you say
Then they ground you for the rest of the day
They always say they're doing what's best for me
And always say, 'We don't agree.'

Mums always talk about you to their mates
Then shout at you when you're 5 minutes late
They say you're cheeky and that you're mean
It's not my fault I'm a terrible teen.

Dads always steal the TV to watch footy
Then scream and shout and drive you nutty
They always want you to do boyish things
And never buy you clothes or earrings.

They tell you off for nothing at all
They embarrass you when your friends call
They make you cook and make you clean
I think they forget I'm only 15.

Sarah Hardy (15)
Eston Park School, Eston

Offensive Bullies, Full Of Hate

Offensive bullies, full of hate
Like unsettled spectres from Hell
Send barrages of brutal words
Harsh,
Hard,
And harmful.

They take advantage of defenceless people
To ruin their lives in school
No reasons are needed,
No questions asked.

Don't they know people can die?
Suicide to escape from the pain
From words,
To kicks,
To death
Don't they know that words hurt?

Isn't there an answer or solution?
A light at the tunnel's end,
Which will finally finish this shadowy journey?
Isn't there a shred of hope?

Sinister,
And ruthless bullies,
Running on the hate and anger from their victims
Liberty,
Is there such a word?
Will the pain ever cease?
Will we ever be free?

Chun Chi Yau (15)
Eston Park School, Eston

The Duel Of The Empire

Shing, the blade went as it was removed from the hilt
His wife was gone, from then his rage built

In the morning sky the blade seemed to glow
Raising the sword for the almighty blow

His challenger dodged and swerved side to side
To stay in one place was like suicide

Steel against steel was like a clash of power
In the mighty shadow of the almighty tower

With quickness of lightning and the skill of the gods
'You cannot win my Lord,' he said, as he started to nod

The king realised his opponent's mistake
The sun was so hot he started to bake

His opponent was tired and with many a flaw
The king set out to settle the score

He brought down his sword and lopped off the head
His opponent was beaten and dropped down dead

The head fell from the neck to the floor
Wiping the sweat from his scared fore.

Joseph Dollery (13)
Eston Park School, Eston

Noise

I like noise
The splodge of people walking through mud,
The whoosh of someone peeling a spud.
The ping of a ball when you hit it with a bat,
The noise of the cards when you're playing snap.
The buzz of a bee when it's collecting honey,
The hiss at the bank when you're collecting money.
The crash of lightning as it hits the ground,
The air doesn't make a sound.
I like noise.

Emma Dawson (11)
Eston Park School, Eston

My Baby

His eyes are bluer than the sky above
His hair blonder than the bright sunny sun
What is this feeling? Is this feeling love?
Tell me should I face it, or should I run?
His smile larger than the whole Earth below
His presence warmer than a nice soft bed
He's there to pick me up when I'm low
He will always be there inside my head
However, he isn't always so nice
Sometimes he can be nasty and evil
And no matter what he does there's a price
If there's something bad to be done - he will!
Despite his downside he's still my baby
And do I love him or not? Well . . . maybe!

Hayley Roxby-Allan (13)
Eston Park School, Eston

Parents

You switch off when they scream and shout,
They ground you so you can't go out,

Don't drink, don't smoke and don't take drugs,
Or you will turn into one of those thugs.

One thing wrong and they see red,
Another and they say you'll be dead,

I know you love me and it's for my own good
Give me some space, if you loved me you would,

I love you too and you have treated me well,
But you were like me at 15 I can tell,

When it's my turn I will know what to do,
I'll be a good parent just like you.

Louise Johnston (15)
Eston Park School, Eston

Free Spirit

Seems so long ago
You were here in my life, happy as can be
Always by my side
Back when you were free
Sprit running free
Spirit riding high
Soaring like the eagle
The spirit will never die
Suddenly you disappeared
Left a void in my life
A gaping hole
Like a cut from a knife
'I'll see you later'
That's what you said to me
'I'll see you later'
You said when you were free
Spirit running free
Spirit riding high
Soaring like the eagle
The spirit will never die

Suddenly I tingle
I turn and you are there
Shivers down my spine
I can only stand and stare
We run to each other
Your battle is done
Together forever
Your freedom is won
Spirit running free
Spirit riding high
Soaring like the eagle
The spirit will never die
'Put the past behind you'
That's what you say to me
We're here together
Now that you are free.

Kate Louise Stephenson (12)
Eston Park School, Eston

Web Of Lies

Have you ever wondered what is out there?
Have you ever wanted to know the truth?
Well . . . the truth is out there, hidden behind
A web of lies conceived by the government.

Anger? No. Only troubled by being misled
I find myself caught in a net of deceit, like a helpless fish.
These conspiracies need to be unveiled.

Think about it.
Did humans really land on the moon?
Was it a basic trick
Like a standard magician on a stage,
To beat the communists in the Cold War?

Will the truth ever be revealed, by them?
'Them' being the misleading government
No, the truth will never come out
It will always be hidden from the public's view.

Carl James (15)
Eston Park School, Eston

My Sonnet

There's a feeling inside that is so strong
It makes me so, so sad to see you cry
My heart beats so fast when you come along
You know my feelings I cannot deny
Can you feel the quick drumming of my heart?
You are my hero with a heart of gold
To know you don't love me tears me apart
My love won't stop even when I grow old.
It hurts me so much to know you don't care
You make it seem as if everything's fine
A feeling so painful it's always there
I can't help but notice your eyes are divine.
I showed you my love as much as I could
Lose my life for you, you know that I would.

Laura Cooke
Eston Park School, Eston

Bullied

Walking to school and the bully stops
Dead in his tracks to look at my watch
He takes it off me and runs away
Into the school to tell his mates.

I walk into school, as fast as I can
But the bully stops in front of me
He has a shining hand
He chucks the watch in front of me
And stands on it vigorously.

I run into the building
And sit on a chair and tell the teacher
Of the bully with no hair
She runs out into the yard
And says 'Who do you think you are?'

I feel like the world has fallen in on me
And all is lost.

Peter Lunn (14)
Eston Park School, Eston

Without You

When we met we had an instant connection,
I knew I liked him, ever since that day,
He seemed to show me a lot of affection,
First of all I didn't know what to say.
His big blue eyes always looking at me,
I can't believe I've liked him for this long,
I thought that then, we were meant to be,
But then suddenly things went wrong.
He then went to live further away,
I knew then I wouldn't see him again,
I was shocked I didn't know what to say,
This bad news left me feeling so much pain.
I wish I could just see him one last time,
To tell him that he will always be mine.

Jodie Fisher (15)
Eston Park School, Eston

Why Did They Pick Me To Bully?

Walking to school worried, they'd better not be there,
Only five minutes to school, I can't see them yet,
They're probably hiding round the corner again,
Why did they pick me to bully, why is it me?

Walking through the gate, as the bell rings they approach,
Clicking their fingers they make me give them money,
Looks like I won't be getting any dinner now,
Why did they pick me to bully, why is it me?

Walking into class late, tears held inside,
People come up to me and ask me what is wrong,
I don't feel well is the only thing that I reply,
Why did they pick me to bully, why is it me?

I'm feeling like a sheep left out of the flock,
Like a failing dove trying to find a friend,
I'm just a loser, who people like to laugh at,
Why did they pick me to bully, why is it me?

It's dinner time now, they'd better not be there,
They're probably spending my dinner money,
I just hope they don't ask for anything more,
Why did they pick me to bully, why is it me?

It's 12.45, nearly time to go in,
They're standing at the gates waiting just for me,
I pluck up my courage and ask them why me?
Why did you pick me to bully, why is it me?

They say because I'm black like the midnight sky,
Bully me because I don't belong in their world,
I'm just a creature that should be hunted down,
That's why they bully me, that's why they do.

Daniel Hutchins (15)
Eston Park School, Eston

Death For No Reason

Locked up in cages
Like prisoners
Forced to take pills, like old people in a home
Cowering in the corner
Of their cage

Dreading when their next experiment will begin
Over two million mice are experimented on each year
That's 5,500 mice, every day
How would *you* like to be experimented on?

How can people inject animals with cancer?
They inject them and watch the cancer grow
Until the cancer is as big as a tennis ball
The animal screams in pain.
And the scientists just watch.

Ainsley Lancaster (15)
Eston Park School, Eston

January

Your eyes are deep pools filling up with fear.
You don't know what else to turn to but death.
Your silent cries that no one else can hear
Are so bad you want to breathe, your last breath
There's no one to talk to; you sit and cry.
No one else understands the pain you feel.
What is going on? I just don't know why
It feels like the world has stopped. But it's real.
You can't go on; there's no one else to blame,
What has caused this? For you to hate your life.
Everyone is hurt and I feel the same.
I can't stop thinking of you with that knife.
I'm always here for you; I hope you know,
We'll always love you and that love will grow.

Laura Allen (15)
Eston Park School, Eston

Hate

Hate can build up inside like a cancer,
It gets so large it becomes hard to control.
Why do you choose to carry this disease?
Take some time out and learn to breathe
If you live to hate you are insecure,
Don't waste your time putting others down.
Instead of carrying all this grief,
Learn to forget and try to move on
Take a look at yourself, be the best you can be
Don't spend the rest of your life hating me.

Rebecca McNeil (15)
Eston Park School, Eston

Secret Love

I saw you standing there, then you saw me
I wonder who knows the way we feel?
As we have a connection, no one can see,
Or that is actually real.
We never really have a lot to say,
You know me probably more than I know you
But that isn't what matters anyway,
And I don't really have a clue.
You're different from anyone else I know,
Even though we know we both lied.
You know the reasons why I am sometimes low,
But we are always trying to hide,
The fact that we can't be together.
But we will remember each other forever.

Lucinda Youngs (15)
Eston Park School, Eston

My Perfect Love

His eyes are deep and dark like the sea-blue sky
His touch is delicate like a flower
His skin so soft and perfect next to me
His love is an everlasting power
The touch of his hand soft and delicate
The words flow nicely from his perfect mouth
The hair on his head, dark and smooth like chocolate
He is unique down from north to the south
His voice flows through the wind to my ears
He looks after me when I am upset
I can tell him my secrets and fears
All this time I have not got one regret
And yet I adore him with all my heart
The rest of my life I never want to part.

Lindsay Robertson (15)
Eston Park School, Eston

First Love

We met and our eyes met we both could see,
Throughout most of the day we did not talk
But your eyes always connected with mine
We spoke that night when we went for a walk
Ever since that day we're never apart.
I love the way that you know me so well
I knew I liked you from the very start.
I know you truly love me, I can tell
Because when I need you, you're always there,
And when I'm upset you can make me smile.
You comfort me and tell me that you care
I don't see you often but it's worthwhile.
Throughout the months I've grown to love you more
You make me happy that's what you're here for.

Amy McBride (15)
Eston Park School, Eston

Demons Of Death

They are sick and twisted with bitter minds,
They kill themselves to cause others pain,
They target us, will we fall to our deaths?
And for what, world domination?

They destroy homes, kill innocent people,
They haunt our minds, what will they do next?
Just like poverty, it never goes away,
The fear of death, in such an inhumane way

What goes through their mind?
How do they think?
These demons of death, what will they bring?
They bring fear to the world, these unpredictable beasts
And for what, their own pleasure?

They can destroy the Earth but what's the point?
What will they gain if they die themselves?
The world would be wasteland, there would be no life,
Nothing left for them to kill.

Sam Rudd (15)
Eston Park School, Eston

We Are The Terrorists

We enter your country without permission
We set up our bombs for a secret mission.

We strap to ourselves, 20 red sticks,
With a push of a button we'll recreate the Blitz

A normal day we'll work in the morning
The terrorists strike without a warning.

We blow up your cities; we blow up your towns,
We blow up your damn so everyone drowns

There was nowhere to run, nowhere to hide
When the terrorists came everyone died.

Robert Carter (13)
Estover Community College, Estover

I Am A Footballer

I am a footballer
Big game is near
Championship decider
Will I shed a tear?

I am a footballer
Walking onto the pitch
The adrenaline pumps
Like a flick of a switch

I am a footballer
My skills are quick
Don't blink
I've done a trick

I am a footballer
The pressure mounts
One-nil down
Everything counts

I am a footballer
80 minutes in
Come on lads!
We can get a win

I am a footballer
Our luck has turned
Round the keeper
It's what we've earned

I am a footballer
1-1 the score
Our luck has changed
We score once more

*I am a footballer
2-1 the score!*

Danny Walton (13)
Estover Community College, Estover

Chocolate

Galaxy
And Milky Way
Lion
And Mars bar
Twirl
And Bueno
Snickers
And Dairy Milk
Double Decker
And Twix
Yorkie
And KitKat
Aero
And chocolate buttons
Smarties
And Toffee Crisp
Toblerone
And Freddo
Curly Wurly
And Chomp
Fudge
And Ripple
Chocolate everywhere
Shining with life
Spread out in front
Of the shop lady
Buy some
And taste the delight!

Jemma Rose (13)
Estover Community College, Estover

The Hand

The hand will get you
It's coming, it's coming
A vicious, fiery hand
But it doesn't live on land

What will it do?
Nobody knows
Where will it go?
Nobody knows

The most vicious
And crafty
Of them all.
With an evil growl.

It's waiting to get you.
What will it look like?
You'll never know.
Until it gets you . . .

Amy Mouncher (13)
Estover Community College, Estover

Spiders

Spiders creep
When I am asleep
Their long hairy legs
I have to pick 'em up
With pegs.

They have loads of eyes
I just want them to *die!*

Jade Pindard (13)
Estover Community College, Estover

Names Of English Football Teams To Be Shouted In A Museum When You're Feeling Bored

Man Utd
Newcastle Utd
Man City
Hull City
Torquay Utd
Rotherham Utd
Norwich City
Stoke City
Arsenal FC
Chelsea FC
Charlton Athletic
Wigan Athletic
Bolton Wanderers
Wycombe Wanderers
Aston Villa
Goal!

Nathan Reed (13)
Estover Community College, Estover

I'm Not Bothered

I'm not bothered when I go blue
When I'm in the snow soaking through!
I'm not bothered when I go red
From being on the sunbed!
I'm not bothered when I go white
When I think I've seen a ghost
But I'm alright.

I am bothered when I go green
When I'm sick and people are mean.

Sammy-Jo Richards (13)
Estover Community College, Estover

We Are The Lions

We are the pride
Every other pride must run and hide.

We are the lions that you must pass
To cross our land, and reach the grass.

We kill the wildebeest, who come on our land
They cross the river, next to our sand.

In the middle of the day, we sit in the shade
Admiring our teeth, they are as sharp as a blade.

At the end of the day, we think of our prey
Which will come in the hunt, or the next day.

Rhys Hooper (13)
Estover Community College, Estover

I Don't Care

I don't mind
When my cheeks go rosy
When somebody finds me
Being very nosy

I don't care
When my nose turns blue
When I'm in the snow
And I'm cold right through

I'm not bothered
When my face turns green
I just had my belly button pierced
And I want to scream!

I now lay in bed
Turning greener and greener
And there it goes
Whoops we need a cleaner!

Becky Atkins (13)
Estover Community College, Estover

Friends

Some have many.
Some don't have any.
They can make you feel good.
They can make you feel bad.
Some are sensible.
Some are mad.

Some leave you out
Some count you in.
Some make you feel
Like you just can't win.

But one thing I know,
They're not worth the trouble,
Most friends out there,
Will just burst your bubble!

Gemma Tully (13)
Estover Community College, Estover

The Battlefield

The sand of the battlefield is drenched in red,
Drained from those who are dead.
Killed by the guns that wouldn't stop
By the enemy that was hidden from sight.
For those who tried to fight so bravely
Have now become part of that blood-drained sand.
For those who survived and ran away
Have an everlasting unhappy smile.
For the next batch of soldiers that pass down this blood-drained sand
Will suffer the same fate by the guns that wouldn't stop
And by the enemy that was hidden from sight.
But if those soldiers do pass down and don't turn back
They will become heroes across the land.

Joe Sherred (13)
Highcliffe School, Christchurch

Poverty

Why is it
We have so much
But people in Africa
Have nothing to touch?

We have diamonds and jewels
And soft beds to lie
They do not even have
A good water supply.

They trudge miles to taps
With flies round their faces
Their homes don't have beds
Their shoes don't have laces.

Their feet are bare
How it must hurt
A blanket to share
They sleep in the dirt.

We have what we want
And still ask for more
Help change their lives
And open a door.

Jenny Higson (11)
Highcliffe School, Christchurch

All Because Of One Man

This man with no heart
Hit the Americans to start
War had started.
All the soldiers on a cart going to the Kwik-E-Mart
Before the voyage abroad
Most of them prayed to the Lord.
Wives and family sitting tight
Because in the end they could be in for a fright
But for some a big delight.

Charles Sugden
Highcliffe School, Christchurch

Method In Madness

This isn't a game.
These people are dead
With the patriotic thoughts
You put in their heads.

And what was it for?
The petrol, you say
Will it pour from their veins
When their bodies turn grey?

And what was it for?
The people you say,
When they are dead on the floor
Is it better that way?

And what was it for?
The weapons to find,
They're oh so important,
We must all be blind.

Did the officers tell you
What happens when you die?
On the long journey over
Did you have time to cry?

You're unique, you know,
You're one of a kind,
But they took that away
And made you one in the line.

And what was it for?
Your children will cry
And what was it for?
It was all for a lie.
And what was it for?
It was all for a lie.

Elizabeth McDonald (14)
Highcliffe School, Christchurch

The War

As we march to war
I ask myself, is this a chore?
Is this my path in life
Or will I end my life by knife?

I see lots of people die
And all the men do is sigh
When the dead will never see their wives
And their life has flashed before our eyes.

The gas it hunts you down
Like a horrific, horrible hound
It has no mercy on the men
The gas it closes you in a pen.

So now you know the truth about war
And you can ask yourself, is this a chore?
Some men that fight
They see these horrific sights.

Gabriella-Rose Cooper (14)
Highcliffe School, Christchurch

The War Of Death

Bang! The bomb fell down
Over the soldiers' heads
Bang! The bomb fell down
And now the soldiers are dead
And then there was no sound
Once the soldiers were dead
All they were was a heap on the ground
No pillow lay beneath their heads.

Nicola-Jayne Hazzard (14)
Highcliffe School, Christchurch

Bang, Bang, That German Shot Me Down!

Above the hills looking down
He is a soldier he never frowns.
With a gun, a powerful gun
He strikes men down like Attila the Hun.
On top of a hill he is a god,
Not a bullet can kill the sod.
His name is feared across the land
He makes odd gestures with his hand.
Killing Jews across the land
All with the power of a mighty hand.
His heart is small and black as night
But nevertheless he was a sight.
Women crying; they are in tears
Their husbands' death did not bring cheers.
Thousands died, gassed I saw
I hate this bloody goddam war.
His name is Hitler, had you not heard
The sound of his death too much for words.

Tom Griffiths (14)
Highcliffe School, Christchurch

War Poetry

Poor women weeping as they pass
Knowing the war was going to last.
Weeping, wailing full of woe
Knowing their husbands had no choice but to go.

His back was straight, his face was stern
As he hoped, he would return.
This war is bad killing people
Before they've had a chance at life,
They're forced to march and join the gruesome strife.

It's such a waste, millions are dead
It's such a waste, what a disgrace.

Emily Millar (14)
Highcliffe School, Christchurch

Atrocity

War, suffering, the difference is unknown
The destruction of life, flesh and bone.
The disaster of the night before
Why oh why did we march off to war?
The horrors of the night before becoming clear
As physical sight begins to disappear.
Snuffed out by poisoned gas
Poisoned gas, poisoned gas brings death en masse,
For those who did not prepare,
Death is waiting to take you into its lair.
Their bodies left on the field to rot.
They were alive and well before that final shot.
All of your honour and glory smashed
With all of your dignity hopelessly trashed.
Say goodnight to peaceful nights
For you will wake with fearful frights.
When memories come flooding back
Of all your fellow mates, never coming back.

Christopher Symons (14)
Highcliffe School, Christchurch

The Impact Of War

Here we go again
Setting off once more
Here to feel pain
As I'm walking out the door
I'm leaving in two hours
To start the tragic war
The sound that makes my eardrums quiver
Also makes my body shiver
As I look up in despair
I see bombs flying through the air
I can feel the anger show on my face
As it does on the rest of the human race.

Leanne Stretton (14)
Highcliffe School, Christchurch

Through The Eyes Of War

As they walk through the doors,
Our lads go off to war.
Happy times are left behind,
For the glory they will not find.
Family and friends will stay and cry,
While our lads go to war and die.
In the trenches we get struck by shells
And all they want is the sound of bells.
While our enemy comes for us,
We will not forget our loss.
They go to war and will not return
But want to come home that's their yearn.
They all die in faithful groups
Treading softly through evil loops.
The sand of the desert is sodden red,
Filled with the longing of our dead.
While they march to their deaths
They carry on and fight for breaths.

Michael Albin
Highcliffe School, Christchurch

Darkened Skies

Off they go again into the deadly sunset
Sunrise bringing another devastating day
Fathers, sons, uncles and brothers
Leaving behind loved ones and mothers
Storming ahead in pain and regret
Thoughts and feelings travelling round their heads
Painfully continuing, there's no turning back
From when the sky is blue until it is black
They fall in agony and are left to die
Struggling to fight back all they can do is try
This is no place for you; this is no place for fun
As they disappear to fight, into the deadly sun.

Ellie Stanton (14)
Highcliffe School, Christchurch

Betrayal And Anguish

You promised to keep me, keep me safe and warm.
Guide me through the shadows, keep me out of harm.

Protect me from all evil, that stalk unyielding eyes.
Shelter me from the wind and keep me from lies.

But what becomes of me when my own heart is torn in two?
You're not my safe, warm home now, but my hard unrenching thorn.

The thorn in my side, the demon that haunts my mind.
You cut of me so deep that it grows bigger over time.

You cannot keep me now, my trust has been dissolved.
Hate is all I feel for you, angry bitter and cold.

Blood fills up my eyes, my hurt cannot be described.
Your promises are now meaningless, your truth, deceitful lies.

In my once warm home of safety, there is a chilling breeze.
A home once full of life and love now ceases to breathe.

How could you betray me, drop me to my death?
How could you betray me, now nothing of me is left?

So then you promised, you gave your word, you'd be there
                                        no matter what,
The torture, pain and suffering, are things I have never forgot!

Is that what your word means, to scare me for all to see?
Cut deep into the surface, of my internal memory?

Lucy Etheridge (15)
Highcliffe School, Christchurch

Surroundings

As I look around at the wet, muddy surroundings
With the thunder rumbling and pounding.
I look at the dead bodies on the floor
And think to myself, *what is all this for?*

All this death and all this pain
And all the clothes covered in bloodstains
And for what? All for money and for power
It makes this glorious war oh so sour.

The sound of gunfire all around
Doesn't make me want to hear a sound.
It makes me question this glorious war
All this blood and all this gore.

I pray to God my children will never witness
All this death and selfishness.
Because I was tricked into believing this war was for good
They did not tell me all they should.

So now I stand here looking at all this death
I pray that all these brave men are now at rest.
I pick up my gun and aim at a German man
And unwillingly help with my country's plan.

Heather Moult (14)
Highcliffe School, Christchurch

My War Poem

At last the sound of the drum,
And the firing of the guns,
War's bloody hand,
Reaches out for that poor man.

Suffering slowly,
Softly fading,
Quietly dying,
Heart stops beating.

Caught in the moment,
I can't let it go,
Falling deeper,
Losing control.

Involved in this action,
Looking death in the eye,
At the end of this torturous war,
The silence whispers by.

The thrill is gone,
There's nothing left
Lying here,
I await my death.

Sarah Di Battista (14)
Highcliffe School, Christchurch

My Last Day At War

War, the place where we lay dying,
Whilst our families at home sit there crying,
We hope we will be returning home,
But we have to keep positive because we do not yet know.
Bang, bang, the guns are fired.
We saw our fellow friends being gassed to death.
I stood in shock, when I saw the bombs being let off
And all of a sudden, my world went completely black.

Emma Cardus (14)
Highcliffe School, Christchurch

Time

Tick-tock, tick-tock, tick-tock,
Time is slow,
And time is fast,
Things have gone,
And things have passed.
Everything you do,
Through and through
Is something to do with time.

You wear it on your wrist,
You see it on the wall,
You might have it in your garden,
And even in your school!
Time goes left and time goes right,
Time goes up and time goes down,
And time will never stop.
Tick-tock, tick-tock, tick-tock.

Lauren Cooper (12)
Highcliffe School, Christchurch

Waiting

I am waiting for you
Waiting in the bush.
I am waiting for you,
Slithering in circles.
Watching for you
My fangs are waiting
To send my venom
Into your defenceless neck.
I am waiting for you
Ready to spring.
To attack repeatedly
My fangs are craving
To sink into your flesh.
And I am Mamba
I am waiting for you.

Samuel Griffiths (12)
Lewis School Pengam, Gilfach

Waiting

I am waiting for you!
My tail wagging,
Like a metronome on a piano's wooden frame.
You'd better watch out
When you walk past me
With your leg limping and lame.
I'm waiting for you!
My eyes sharp
As a snake's fang
If you walk past me
You will be gone . . . *bang!*
I am waiting for you!
Soon you'll be in my jaws
Gripped as tight as a vice
Your blood will be down my face
All tasty and nice
I am waiting for you!
I can't wait to have one glimpse of your
Mouth-watering flesh
All that will be left of you
Are your bones
Like a wire mesh
I am wolf
My eyes yellow as amber traffic lights
I am waiting for you!

Josh Joshua (12)
Lewis School Pengam, Gilfach

Garden Brawl

I am waiting for you
Now down by the old plum tree,
To whack you, *smack, bang!*
When you're making a puddle on me.

I am waiting for you down by the shed,
I shall stop this business
Of you kicking me in the head.

I'm getting too old,
I'm beginning to crack up,
So leave me alone, be gone,
You stupid old pup.

I may be small,
Tiny in fact,
But that doesn't mean you can treat me,
Like an old circus act.

I'm thinking of any possible way
Before you come back from your holiday.
I don't want to hurt you, but this abuse has got to stop,
One smart move
And one of your bones will go *pop!*

I'm waiting for you all alone,
Bring it on,
But believe me; you don't want to mess with this garden gnome!

Joseph Leach (12)
Lewis School Pengam, Gilfach

As You See Me

As you see me
Glass shatters and bursts into a million pieces.
Sparkling as if to laugh at me.
But to cry as I fall to the floor.
Lying, not moving as blood drips from my skull.

As you see me
I fell like getting shot between the eyes.
Going down, falling to the ground
Police asking questions, nobody answers for me.
Getting taken away and everyone saying they didn't care.

As you see me
You think I'm soft
So you try and hurt me
But what's the point
As you try to pick a fight
I just walk away,

Ashley Court (11)
Lewis School Pengam, Gilfach

Waiting For You

I'm waiting for you
I'm as quiet as a ghost
I lay on the seabed
I'm getting hungry
So hurry up and feed me
I'm getting really starving
Ah ha! Here you come
Now I will eat you
For I am revealed
I am a shark
And you are my prey.

Sam Forrest (12)
Lewis School Pengam, Gilfach

Waiting For You

I am waiting for you
Come out, come out
Wherever you are
Just come out
I am waiting like a tiger
Waiting to grab you
From your home
And eat you.

I am waiting for you
Like a teacher
Ready to give you detention
I am getting impatient
Like a hunter
Having no luck
Waiting for his prey
Come out, come out, you can't hide from me.

I am waiting for you
I'm coming to your home
I'm coming, coming, coming
Now I've got you
Aah! I like a good bogey
In the morning
Lovely!
He was good!
I'll get the rest later
Ha, ha, ha!

Alex Williams (13)
Lewis School Pengam, Gilfach

The Creature

As the sun sets in the west,
I noticed something on my chest.
It moved like an elderly snail,
But was as elegant as chain-mail.

Its small, dark horns, razor-sharp,
With the face of a carp.
Four legs attached to a body,
I turn my head and there is Noddy!

There he is in his bright blue hat,
While I'm being attacked by a scary bat!

Suddenly I wake with a fright,
Just to find it's the middle of the night.
I turn on the TV, to find that I'm blind,
Then I think, *God you're not kind.*

Gareth Griffiths (12)
Lewis School Pengam, Gilfach

Waiting

I'm waiting for you in the snow
I'm big and white, you'd better not go.
My claws are sharp; they'll pierce your skin,
Like a sewing machine or a razor-sharp pin.

I'm waiting for you to come into my reach,
I'll suck your blood, just like a leach.
I'll eat your flesh and bury your bones,
Just like a lion, under the stones.

Ben Clark (12)
Lewis School Pengam, Gilfach

Waiting For You

I am waiting for you
In the deep dark ocean
Waiting like a tiger
About to pounce
I am waiting for you
You little fish
Able to swim about fast
I am waiting for you
When you swim past me
I will tear your body apart
You will live no more
I am waiting for you
Watch your back
You might just
Be caught by me
I am a shark
Waiting for you.

David Shenton (12)
Lewis School Pengam, Gilfach

Waiting For You

I'm waiting for you
Precious
My body, black
Like a storm
Sleek and slim
My claws
Like a razor
Can rip you
To shreds
Aah!
I am a panther!

Nathan Hazell (12)
Lewis School Pengam, Gilfach

The Roller Coaster

Adrenalin and blood pumping through my heart,
My pulse was beating wildly,
As the coaster went round like a dart.

The speed and immensity
Of the speeding ride,
The greatness and immensity
Of the structure inside.

Round and round the coaster goes
Like a falling plane,
You're fearsome, everybody knows
Like a lion's mane.

To a halt the ride eventually comes
Slowly but surely it arrives
Sickened to the stomach are some
But I feel so alive.

Rhys Owens (12)
Lewis School Pengam, Gilfach

The War Story

I am waiting for you
Darth Nihilus.
You cannot do me any damage
I am a Jedi master onto you.
As you arrive I will challenge you
You will fall.
I will end you with a striking blow.
You will lose everything.
The Empire should be very afraid.
They will crumble.
And they will be sent to Hell.
Finally we will have brought balance
To the Force.

Lee Knicz (12)
Lewis School Pengam, Gilfach

Senses Poem

I am walking in the woods
Hearing leaves being thrown about
Hearing birds chirping
Hearing squirrels darting about the place.

Feeling the rough bark of trees
Feeling the squelchy mud underneath my feet
Feeling the raindrops slowly coming down.

Tasting the texture of the air
Tasting wild strawberries
Tasting raindrops hitting me in the mouth.

Smelling the wet, thick, dark, sticky mud
Smelling animals' droppings over the squelchy floor
Smelling the wet disturbed leaves.

Seeing the gigantic ancient trees
Seeing birds and squirrels
Seeing footprints in the mud.

Matthew Powell (12)
Lewis School Pengam, Gilfach

The Poet With No Name

The poet with no name,
Sat in his dark, dank office,
Next to his old, worn desk
This writer wasn't though
Wasn't the same.

The poet who had no name,
Had no glory, destiny or fame
He sat all alone
With his head bowed in shame.

The poet who had no name
Did
It was Jeroy.

Blake Edwards (12)
Lewis School Pengam, Gilfach

I Am Waiting For You

I am waiting for you
To step into my sights,
I will pin you down
With my bullets,
Like a tiger,
After its prey.
With my gun in my hands,
My fingers resting
On the trigger,
Waiting,
For the precise moment
To shoot you,
To end your life
Forever.
Once you enter my view,
I will pull back the trigger
And make you suffer,
I will wait for you,
Like a polar bear
After a shoal of fish.
I will hunt you down
Until the end,
I will bring you down
I'm waiting for you!

Jake Elliott (12)
Lewis School Pengam, Gilfach

Waiting For You

I'm waiting for you,
In the cold, cruel night,
I'm coming to get you,
Prepare for a fright!
It's Friday 13th
It's time to die,
I'll creep up on you,
Like a fox; dead sly!

Unsuspecting you walk on,
You stop, then carry on,
I'm going to tear you,
Flesh from bone,
And as you die,
You lightly moan,
'He was waiting for me,'
But I was,
Waiting for you!

Adam Vile (12)
Lewis School Pengam, Gilfach

Waiting

I am waiting for you,
I want to eat you up.
I am waiting for you
I want to eat you up.
I want to move in
For the kill.
When you come
I will, I will.
You'd better watch out
Because I'm as silent as a trout.
Really, all you should know
Is that I'm waiting for you,
I am tiger,
Waiting for you.

Amar Ali (11)
Lewis School Pengam, Gilfach

Get On Your Bike!

Sliding your helmet on,
With the race about to begin
Your heart pounding in your ears
Butterflies in your stomach.

There is a field of crop
Next to which the gate's about to drop
Everyone's getting ready
The World Championship is at stake.

The gate's dropped!
You snap the bike out
Down into the first set of jumps
Round the turn, into the lead!

Pump the jump, still in the lead!
Round the S-bend, someone's catching up
Style the jump and another
Over the final jump with a one-footer,
You've won!

Liam Shaughnessy (12)
Lewis School Pengam, Gilfach

I Am Waiting For You

I'm waiting for you like a shark in the deep
Submerged in the deep
Like a car at a stoplight
I'm waiting for you.

I am waiting in the thick vast savannah
Lurking behind a rock
I'll wait all night if I have to
To drag you behind my rock.

Ben Rees (12)
Lewis School Pengam, Gilfach

Waiting For You

I am waiting for you,
To fall into my trap,
Waiting patiently
Like a boy
Waiting for the bell to ring.
My tail is waggling
My teeth are waiting
To rip you apart.
My tongue is ready
To taste you,
Your blood.
I am an enormous creature
Living in the sea,
My eyes are looking
Very furious
Just waiting for you,
I am a shark
And suddenly I've got him!

Calum Duncan (12)
Lewis School Pengam, Gilfach

The Graveyard

The shadowy gravestones towered above my head
As I walked along the sinister shadows they gave,
I was quiet; it felt rude to break the silence of the dead,
The place was so creepy it sent shivers all down me,
Eventually I found the grave I had been searching for,
I came to pay my respects so I knelt down on one knee,
Although it was midday it was terribly dark around here
I looked up to see a canopy of dead leaves blocking the sun,
The sadness of the last weeks made my eyes fill,
                              out came a single tear.

Lizzie Clark (12)
Penryn College, Penryn

This Place Is Only A Dream

I have always dreamt of a place
A place where there is no war,
Where no one is hungry or suffering.
A place where no one is poor,
I wish for a place with no racism,
Who cares if you're black or white?
What religion you are does not matter,
For inside we are all alike.
This paradise I dream of,
This place which is unseen,
This heaven here on Earth,
This place is only a dream.
I imagine a world where no child,
Fears that soon they shall surely die,
From starvation or physical cruelty,
In my world there's no need to cry.
I dream of a place where the elderly
Are confident to walk out at night,
For in my world there would be
No thugs or drunken fights.
This paradise I dream of,
This place which is unseen,
This heaven here on Earth,
This place remains a dream!

Sancha Annear (12)
Penryn College, Penryn

My Poem Under The Sea

Deep under the sea,
Darts a fish that looks like a bee,
Swerving so fast,
You'll only glimpse him swim past.

Deep under the sea lurks a huge whale,
Its fin alone is as big as a sail,
But the animals it eats are so tiny and small,
You would think at that size it would eat something tall.

Deep under the sea lying on the rocks
Is a beautiful starfish covered in spots,
Red, yellow, orange and blue,
The colour they are might surprise you.

Deep under the sea dolphins glide,
As they swim from side to side,
Happy dolphins love to play,
They can stay smiling for the whole day.

Deep under the sea is a baby seal,
She waits for her mother collecting her meal,
Down under rocks she will slide
From bigger fish she must hide.

Deep under the sea a crab is side-walking,
It would scuttle away if it heard you talking,
Pinching claws are its defence,
So fish stay away if they have any sense.

But under the sea is someone not so calm,
The sight of his jaws causes alarm,
His sharp teeth in many rows,
So stay away everyone knows,
Searching for a fish meal is he,
Maybe he'll eat the one that looks like a bee!

Gabby Moore (13)
Penryn College, Penryn

Randomise

Football is so great,
I play it most of the time,
The only reason I wrote this,
Is so I could make it rhyme.

You may think I'm weird,
But I don't really care,
At this present moment in time,
I'm wearing dark blue underwear.

Cricket's rather fun,
I play it now and then,
My granny is completely crazy,
And my friend's uncle is called Glen.

Skating surfer dudes are wicked,
But only when they bust sick tricks,
My favourite move is the banana flip,
But my worst shop is Wickes.

Your dad looks like a baboon,
One with a big red ass,
Your mum looks like a hippo,
One with a very large mass.

You look like a rat,
One that lives in a sewer,
The sky is very blue,
But the sea is even bluer.

Hal Parsons (13)
Penryn College, Penryn

Palm Tree Paradise

White-tipped waves die on the sandy shore
The huge red sun resting on the edge of the world
Wheeling and squealing the gulls search for their evening meal,
As I walk along the beautiful beach,
I feel sand sifting through my toes.
This is my palm tree paradise!

Palm trees wave farewell to the sun
In the distance, white sails head for home,
A large ship pollutes the air
A flicker of light catches my eye
It watches over us as the sun slowly disappears.
This is my palm tree paradise!

Movement out in the deep blue sea, fast and quick
Elegant as ballerinas
Wildly weaving through the waves without a whisper
As more appear I count ten, eleven and twelve
Free as a bird.
This is my palm tree paradise!

Cat Dove (13)
Penryn College, Penryn

Football Crazy!

Football crazy, football mad
Grab a pair of boots and play football with the lads.

Man United and Arsenal in the Premiership,
They go along doing loads of football tricks.

With Swansea and Wrexham in the bottom league,
They are going down, not in the lead.

Football crazy, football mad
Grab a pair of boots and play football with the lads.

Louis Assiratti (12)
Radyr Comprehensive School, Cardiff

The Second World War

It started with a bang,
The crackle of rifle fire rang.
It rang through Poland and its borders.
It came from German army soldiers.
Hitler had broken his word as well as the Polish army.
Chamberlain had responded calmly.
He signed a piece of paper.
The British public said, 'See you later.'
In came Winston Churchill.
He quickly passed the 'Call To Arms Bill' in December 1941.
The Americans were lying in the sun
When it all began.
The decks emptied as they ran
The Japanese bombers came in.
Their bombs as deadly as sin.
Most of the ships were sunk.
All that was left at the bottom was a pile of junk.
As well as the countless numbers of dead sailors.
This all happened because the incoming bombers
Weren't announced on the loud hailers.
The Battle of Britain was the largest air battle ever fought.
Over fifty German pilots were caught.

Matthew Learoyd (12)
Radyr Comprehensive School, Cardiff

Sweet World

Creamy and smooth milk chocolate,
Swirling round and round,
In a giant swimming pool,
Making an inviting sound.

I dive right in,
Fully clothed,
Slurping up this treat,
The chocolate's going everywhere,
Splashed by my kicking feet.

Houses standing everywhere,
Made of bourbons and custard creams,
You'd think this place only existed,
In little children's dreams.

Cars zooming around the backstreets,
Weaving in and out,
Made of dollops of ice cream,
They make me want to shout.

I wish this place would never end,
I like this place so much,
I really don't want to go home yet,
I just want to munch.

Matthew Smith (12)
Radyr Comprehensive School, Cardiff

The Mouse In The House

The mouse is brown and white,
He doesn't know what's wrong or right.
He searches the house day and night.
He doesn't go without a fight.
He lives in a hole down under the stairs.
You can find him from his trail of hairs.

Alex Coombes (12)
Radyr Comprehensive School, Cardiff

My Favourite Thing . . .

My favourite thing is my cat,
He is called Jess,
He is the best.

We saw him first under a chair,
All he did was sit and stare,
He calmed down after a while
And played around which made us smile.

Jess is black and white,
He had a rather big fright,
When he chased a bird in flight.

He loves wet food,
And doesn't like the dry,
He especially loves the special milk you can buy.

Our cat has bitten our dad's hand,
And has torn the pouffe to shreds,
He chases cats and bites tiny voles' heads.

Jess loves to have a nap,
On my lap,
And that's the story of my favourite cat.

Kim Howcroft (13)
Radyr Comprehensive School, Cardiff

World War II

Armoured tanks driving through town,
Nazi aircrafts getting shot down.
Everywhere closed off by the military
Soldiers supported by the infantry.
The death toll is rising every day
Someone in this war is going to pay.
How long it will last? Nobody knows,
People now use missiles, instead of crossbows.
'War is terrible,' I hear you say,
It started in July and now it's May.

Marc Tilley (12)
Radyr Comprehensive School, Cardiff

The Monster Under My Bed

'Please don't make me!' I pleaded,
'I do homework that's needed!'
'Now don't fuss,' my mother said,
'You have to go to bed.'

'My bed,' I cried, 'is one I share'
'Why?'
'There's a monster under there!'
'Don't be silly, that room is a pig sty and don't be shy.'

I went upstairs into my room
I looked around in the messy gloom,
Nothing was there, or so I thought,
Things aren't always what they seem, I was taught.

'See, nothing there,' she smiled,
But I could see something wild,
The green eyes glowed,
And then I knew.

'Rooaaar!' It roared,
And it soared
Towards my mother and me,
It stopped in mid pounce as still as could be.

It flew out the window
Made a show,
Into the neighbour's room
'See,' Mother smiled 'they always go with a boom!'

The next minute what I heard
Was like an explosion occurred
The monster had gone,
But I will see him again and it won't be long.

Amy Wiggins (12)
Radyr Comprehensive School, Cardiff

The Sun

A grand gigantic sphere of fire
Slowly piercing the clouds and bursting through.
It's horrendously hot
Its brightness is unbearable
You can't even look at it
If you do, I'll warn you
It will make your eyes blur.

As the heat hits my face
A splendid warmth runs through me
As if I was leaning on a radiator
A bead of water trickles down my back
Like a raindrop on a windowpane.

Everyone so happy
Now the sun is out
From these past rainy days
I suppose it's nice to have a change
I can hear children playing outside
What a nice surprise
The ice cream van chimes
Calls all children
A huge queue for ice cream
A fresh, cooled ice cream
It will be worth the wait.

Screaming, shouting, playing
Can now be heard down the street
The joy of children's laughter
Now that the sun is out!

Sara Howell (12)
Radyr Comprehensive School, Cardiff

School

The sound of the school bell
We're on our way to Hell.
Our first lesson's art
Poor Benji did a fart.
We all thought it was very funny
But the teacher gave him a B3.
Our next lesson's history, it's really fun
But the maths teacher's coming so run, run, run!
We're learning about the Middle Ages, it's very boring,
Matthew sitting next to me has started snoring.
Now we're on our way to French
Marc broke the doorknob with a large wrench.
Everyone but Matthew said, 'Bonjour,'
But Matthew just gave a very loud snore.
Now it's time for lunch in the canteen,
Marc tried to sneak in without being seen.
He always gets caught and would always mention
'That teacher on duty gave me a detention!'
We have English period four,
We all trooped in through the door.
I didn't hear the bell and I was late
I came in five minutes through the civil debate.
Our IT teacher has grey hair
He gave me a B1 for swinging on my chair.
Matthew turned off the computer before he was told
But the teacher didn't notice because he is very old.
Now I'm going home on the bus
There is no room but I'm not making a fuss.
I had a really good day in school, it was so fun
Oh no, the maths teacher, run, run, run!

Huw Lewis (12)
Radyr Comprehensive School, Cardiff

Summer

Sassy, sunny summer.
Sit back and enjoy my poem about summer.
Think back to yesteryears when leg warmers and Afros
                                        were in fashion.

Sassy, sunny summer.
When the skies are blue and clear,
Oh bummer, it's not gonna last all year.
Everyone so alive and shining with glee,
But the wasps and fleas are missing scones and tea.

Sassy, sunny summer.
I look forward to it all year round,
When cheeky kids' ice creams drip on the ground.
Summer is the best season you've got to admit,
It's the best, better than the rest,
Sassy, sunny summer.

Emily Donnan (12)
Radyr Comprehensive School, Cardiff

School

School can be fun
Because you get to see your friends.

But when it comes to lesson time
It gets boring in the end.

I like it when it's break time
Because you get to chat and eat.

Lunchtime is the best
But dinner isn't free.

Half past three is time to go
Yippee! Oh Mummy, I am home.

Olivia Beere (11)
Radyr Comprehensive School, Cardiff

My Favourite Thing Is . . .

My favourite thing is my cat,
He is white and black.
He sits on my lap,
And is not very fat.

We bought him from the RSPCA,
When we went to have a look in the day.
It said on the box that he was shy,
But when we got him home he was as playful as a cat which
                                                                      wanted to fly.

First of all we chose another cat with a blind eye,
But its blood pressure was high,
So it might die,
Sadly we had to say goodbye.

Jess never drinks a drop of water,
But we think he oughta.
Jess likes the wet cat food,
If we gave him the other he would go into a mood.

Once Jess brought home a vole,
It was the colour of coal,
Dad put it in the bin,
The person who was sad about it was Kim.

Guy Howcroft (13)
Radyr Comprehensive School, Cardiff

Chocolate

I love chocolate,
When it's sweet and creamy,
Milky and ever so dreamy.
Giant Smarties, Milky Way bars,
Cadbury's caramel and king-size Mars
Dark chocolate, white chocolate,
Milk chocolate too!
Chocolate is my favourite food!
I love chocolate!

Loren Evans (12)
Radyr Comprehensive School, Cardiff

My Dog

Oh I love him,
I love him very much,
He is small, he is cuddly,
And very, very soft.

If you give him food,
He will do as you please,
He will jump, he will sit,
He will jump onto your knees!

If you take his ball,
He will bark very much,
He will ask, he will plead,
He will beg at your feet!

He doesn't like cats,
He is very, very playful,
His name is Eddie,
And he is my dog!

Natasha Shorte (13)
Radyr Comprehensive School, Cardiff

Sport

I love sport, it is the best,
Swimming, netball, tennis and the rest.
I love sport,
Yes I do and you should too!
You should do it every day,
Not sitting in when you could go out and play.
Sport, sport, it's so great
It makes you get fit and you will then look great.
Sport, sport, sport, it is the best,
Better than all the rest!

Eleanor Baxter (12)
Radyr Comprehensive School, Cardiff

School!

School can be boring,
School can be fun,
School can be interesting,
School can be glum.

History, English, geography, art,
Science, maths, drama,
All that counts is the taking part.

School can be boring,
School can be fun,
When it comes to dinner time,
Everybody starts to run.

History, English, geography, art,
Science, maths, drama,
All that counts is the taking part.

School can be boring,
School can be fun,
Soon it'll be time to leave,
And have fun in the sun!

Louise Edmunds (13)
Radyr Comprehensive School, Cardiff

My Favourite Sport

My favourite sport makes you feel as free as a bird.
My favourite sport makes me think I am the best.
My favourite sport makes you glide over the ground like
                                    a swan on water.
My favourite sport makes the wind run through my hair
As quick as a runner over the track.
My favourite sport makes you feel fit and strong
Even though it hurts!
My favourite sport is cycling!

Hannah Manley (12)
Radyr Comprehensive School, Cardiff

Solva

Green luscious grass,
Sapphire-blue sky,
Red roaring dragon,
Golden glowing sun
Children having fun!

Beautiful still harbour,
Boats bob up and down,
Loud crashing waves
Paddle at the shore,
Looking for some more!

In the fields of the countryside,
The cows and sheep will graze,
Farmers working hard all day,
Growing food for us to eat,
Oh what a treat!

All of these wonderful things,
Describe my favourite place,
Sun, sand, sea and sails,
The place - Solva, West Wales!

Charlotte Rees (13)
Radyr Comprehensive School, Cardiff

Yuck!

Dead, rotting mice
Don't taste too nice.

Mouldy, hard cheese
Makes me more than sneeze.

Black, curled skin,
Best put it in the bin.

Bruised, gross bananas,
Grown by rubbish farmers.

All these things make me go yuck!

Tom Heyman (11)
Radyr Comprehensive School, Cardiff

The Box That Took Over The World

They sit in front of it every day,
It prevents them from going out to play.

There's so much more to do out there,
Than just to sit and glare.

When they should be exercising,
Or maybe even doing some revising,
All they do is lounge around,
Looking blank and making no sound.

Won't anyone see what these things really are?
They're evil; you can even get them in cars.

Guessed what I'm talking about yet?
Yep, it's the television set!

Arran Coe (13)
Radyr Comprehensive School, Cardiff

Our World

The green, green grass,
The yellow, yellow stars,
The orange, orange sun,
Is what makes life fun!

The purply-pink flowers,
That grow through the hours,
Each and every day through the sun and rain
No matter what it is, it takes away the pain!
From monkeys to sheep,
We all need to sleep,
So I'm going to say goodbye
And let you guess why!

Rhys Laskcy (13)
Radyr Comprehensive School, Cardiff

My Poem
(Based on 'Macbeth')

Double trouble toil and bubble, *fire burn and cauldron bubble.*
Three dead bodies fresh from their grave,
The arm of a pyramid's slave.
A dead rotting shark from the ocean,
This will be the first part of the potion.

Double trouble toil and bubble, *fire burn and cauldron bubble.*

One fish you shall boil,
And bury it in rich soil.
A bird of prey and a baby mouse,
All the people of a rich house.

Double trouble toil and bubble, *fire burn and cauldron bubble.*

Take from an old bird, twenty-one feathers,
Murder a carpenter and steal all his leather.
Find a lizard with a blue tongue,
Then the fin of a dolphin, make sure it's young.

Double trouble toil and bubble, *fire burn and cauldron bubble.*

Ali Emad Jaffery (13)
Radyr Comprehensive School, Cardiff

Sunny Summer

The sun is shining
Like a really bright torch
As I stand in my front porch.

The sun is bright
Like a very bright light
Like a lighthouse
Shining on the sea waters.

The sun is gleaming
During the summer it gleams
It sends out beams of light like a laser.

Jared Hughes (13)
Radyr Comprehensive School, Cardiff

My Caterpillar

Once I saw a caterpillar,
It wriggled across the floor.
Climbed upon a leaf
And I saw it no more.

I saw the caterpillar again today,
And picked it off the ground.
Took it home in a box,
Without making a sound.

I called my caterpillar Lettuce,
Because that's all it eats.
It's started to get a little fatter,
And grown a few more feet.

My caterpillar's looking strange,
It's started to go brown.
My mum says it's a cocoon,
And there's no need to frown.

The cocoon is even bigger now,
It's started to crack.
Soon there will be a butterfly,
Coming out of this brown sack.

I looked back in the box today,
And noticed the caterpillar gone.
I saw a butterfly by the window,
And cried for ever so long.

My beautiful baby caterpillar,
Is now flying about.
I realised it's time to let go,
And let my beautiful baby butterfly out.

Sallyann Moore (13)
Radyr Comprehensive School, Cardiff

Chocolate

You eat it when you feel good,
You eat it when you're down.
You eat it wearing a smile,
You eat it wearing a frown.

You eat it when in love,
You eat it when in lust.
You eat every single piece,
Even crumbs and dust.

You'll eat it after school,
You'll eat it on a weekend.
You'll eat it on a holiday,
Or when you're driven round the bend.

You'll eat it at a party,
You'll eat it at a fête.
You'll share it with your friends,
But not the ones you hate.

You'll eat it when it's cold,
On a frozen Christmas Day.
You'll eat it when the sun is out,
On a peaceful day in May.

You'll eat it doing homework,
You'll eat it doing chores.
You'll eat it being grounded,
But from behind closed doors.

Chocolate makes you feel good,
Even when you're down.
It helps you make a smile,
Out of a frown.

Amy Jenkins (13)
Radyr Comprehensive School, Cardiff

Golf

Today I play golf by myself
Carefully putting my ball onto the tee
Staying calm I swing the club
Sweeping it off the tee and into the sky
Look at that, it's as straight as a die.
What a shot onto the green
The best shot I have ever seen.
The green grass twinkles in my eye
Please don't miss it or I'll cry
I stand to the ball making my line
I nod my head, that is fine.
Moving the club I hit the ball
'Come on!' I will call
Oh yeah! I'm on a roll
That's it baby, in the hole!

Lewis Jones (13)
Radyr Comprehensive School, Cardiff

Ocean Breeze

The crashing waves bellow before her feet,
The sunshine glows on her golden hair.
Her sun-kissed skin is as smooth as pebble
And she stares beyond the deep blue sea.

She wades through the seaweed,
Which lies on the shore.
She paddles into the deserted ocean,
Where the waves roar and crash.

In the distance she can see it,
It is the perfect waves.
The breeze blows on her face,
And she flies through the ocean with the wave.

Megan Burford (13)
Radyr Comprehensive School, Cardiff

My Life

My life is like a strange creature,
Put on show for all to see.
Given a label like, 'weird freak',
Like the Loch Ness Monster or a Harpie.

Known as evil, crazy and psychotic,
Being told to burn in Hell.
So what, I like murder and demons,
And love a guy who lives in a cell.

It's nice to stand out and be one in a crowd,
Instead of following the herd.
It's worse to be known as 'Chav' or 'Prep',
Bring a rocker means free as a bird.

So Guns 'n' Roses live on,
And Nirvana still rocks.
At least they're all legends,
Unlike all these jocks.

Rhiannon Jones (14)
Radyr Comprehensive School, Cardiff

Camping

Camping round a fire,
Stars overhead.
Sounds and shadows,
No warm bed.

Rustling trees,
Sing you to sleep.
Just you and the stars,
And a field full of sheep.

James Longville (13)
Radyr Comprehensive School, Cardiff

My Teacher

Mrs Fowler is my teacher,
She teaches me English.
But I don't know why she does it,
Because I will never go to England.

She teaches very well,
And she is kind of strict.
But when you get used to her,
She is really kind of neat.

Now that is my poem about my teacher,
I hope you all enjoyed.
But if you do not like it,
I will really be annoyed.

Rebekah Ellis (13)
Radyr Comprehensive School, Cardiff

Life Is What You Make It

Life is like a see-saw
It rocks you up and down.
Sometimes it makes you happy
Sometimes it spins around.

Life can be so boring,
But can always be made fun.
You can be really happy,
You can be really glum.

But life is what you make it,
So be positive and kind.
Don't be sad, depressed, unhappy,
Your life depends on your mind.

Sam Lyle (13)
Radyr Comprehensive School, Cardiff

Summer!

I love summer,
The heat of the golden, sizzling sun,
The smell of the freshly cut green grass,
The sound of the crashing waves,
The taste of creamy, cold ice cream,
I love summer!

The sun rises in the sapphire-blue sky,
Me and my mates head down to the beach,
Lots of big birds fly by,
As we all head down to the beach.

Water fights,
Water bombs,
Barbecues and fun,
Yes summer is finally here,
So come on everybody let's hear you cheer!

Megan Price (13)
Radyr Comprehensive School, Cardiff

Stop War

This is where lives are lost,
This is where innocent people die,
This is where you may never rest,
Never be in peace.

This is where you lie under a dark blanket,
With no freedom.

This is your worst nightmare,
This is war.

It's time to make peace,
Time to save lives.

Give people freedom,
Let them be happy.

Time to stop war!

Lewis Simpson (13)
Radyr Comprehensive School, Cardiff

My Pets

I love my pets I really do,
They make me happy when I'm blue.
Shadow is big, black and strong,
Abbey is little but still tags along.
I open the gate and out they run,
Throwing the ball having so much fun.
They are there every day,
I hope they never go away.

They protect me when I'm alone,
And if they're good they get a bone.
When I hug them their fur tickles me,
But when they scratch it stings like a bee.
Their eyes brim with happiness and joy,
I treat them with a bone or a toy.
I love my pets I really do,
They make me happy when I'm blue.

Charlene Simmonds (14)
Radyr Comprehensive School, Cardiff

Zilch Badger

Kris is my name,
Zilch is my nickname,
Jumping past some steps,
It was just a quick game.
Ten, five, then it was naught,
Let's call him Zilch, someone thought.

Then they called me Badger,
It was quite clever!
A black hair colour,
And I'm a white-skinned fella!
And so the name's Zilch Badger,
Please . . . try and remember!

Kristian Matthews (13)
Radyr Comprehensive School, Cardiff

Growing, Cooking, Eating

Farmers help our food to grow,
Potatoes, carrots and marrow.
As he takes it through his gate,
It will soon be on his plate.

We wash them first to remove the soil,
Before we put them on to boil.
Cooking food is sometimes fun,
Rumble, grumble goes my tum!

Cooking food can be an art,
But eating it's my favourite part.
As I sit eating my jelly,
I feel it sliding into my belly!

Jemma Flynn (14)
Radyr Comprehensive School, Cardiff

The Sun

The sun is a gold coin in a purse,
The sun is orange juice in a glass,
The sun is a melon on a sunny day,
The sun is a ginger cat down a dark alley.

The rain is a shower,
The rain is a water fountain,
The rain is a spurt of water,
The rain is a splash of water from a swimming pool.

The snow is ice cream in a bowl,
The snow is icing sugar on a cake,
The snow falling is like a football flying through the air,
The snow in view is like a white board.

Daryl Murray (14)
Radyr Comprehensive School, Cardiff

The Welsh Dragon

The blood-red dragon is a symbol of Wales,
The big fierce dragon tells many tales,
Its huge chunky jaws snap and bite,
The fearsome dragon puts up an awesome fight,
Its long scaly tail swishes back and forth,
If you get on the wrong side of him
He will let out a terrifying roar,
The dragon's big open eyes tell a spine-tingling story,
It's about bravery and fear and the Welsh glory.

Sam Langford (14)
Radyr Comprehensive School, Cardiff

I Love Greece

I love Greece,
The weather is hot,
I like it a lot,
As I swim in the sea,
I get so refreshed,
It's forty degrees,
Still good for me,
Just go for another,
Swim in the sea.

The sea is clear,
Even after a year,
It's crystal clear,
Just like the bubbles in a beer,
I can't wait to go again,
Because I will see my friend.

Themis Zafiropoulos (14)
Radyr Comprehensive School, Cardiff

Journey Of Life

An endless journey of breathtaking madness,
The need for ups and downs,
A balance of both wealth and health,
A long trek of survival,
But the most puzzling of all, decisions.

Strengths and weaknesses make it hard,
Especially when we don't often stay strong,
Trying hard may not lead to success,
But effort should be taken into account.
As those who don't attempt, may be the ones to doubt.

Hold the treasured memories within your heart,
As we don't know the meaning of all this.
It's what to expect with life,
Take it as it comes,
Forget the past, live for the future,
Upon the journey of life.

Ceri James (14)
Radyr Comprehensive School, Cardiff

Hide, For The Storm Is Here

I hear a gre at storm coming across the land,
The thunder is deafening and the lightning is bright,
But all I want to do is sleep,
But through the thunder and lightning, I can't sleep but weep.

I hide under the cover then gasp for breath,
The storm is getting worse and the noise is hell,
All I can do is wait,
Until the day is dawning.

Rowan Axe (14)
Radyr Comprehensive School, Cardiff

Countryside

The countryside is a beautiful place
Which contains a lot of things.

There are trees that are tall, short, skinny or fat,
You climb them branch by branch.

There's fresh green grass which is neatly trimmed
Like a barber cutting your hair.

There are flowers everywhere in lots of different colours,
With a long green stem which makes the flowers tall.

The countryside is a beautiful place,
Especially in the fall.

Mercedes Ttophi (14)
Radyr Comprehensive School, Cardiff

The End Of The Year!

It's that final time again,
We're now at the end of Year 9.
Although the teachers were a pain,
Everybody seemed to get on fine.

We've done our SATs,
And options too.
We all deserve 'well done' hats!
For all the hard work we've done for you.

We've done the summer sizzler,
And the sponsored run.
We've eaten our turkey twizzler,
And are ready to have fun.

Katie Haskell (14)
Radyr Comprehensive School, Cardiff

A Lion's Delight

I am waiting for you,
My juicy, salty meat.
I'll rip you and bite you,
Dribbling as I eat.

I am waiting for you,
A lion's delight.
It lives on a farm,
It's chicken tonight.

I am waiting for you,
A five star dish.
One of my favourites
It has to be fish.

I am waiting for you,
No knife or fork.
Sausage and bacon,
Bring me the pork.

I am waiting for you,
The variety, the mixture.
But succulent beef,
Is a lion's elixir!

Ryan Jenkins (12)
Radyr Comprehensive School, Cardiff

Year 9 Poems

Year 9 poems are hard to write
They usually keep me up all night
Thinking of just what to say
In the perfect rhyming way
This one was different, slipped into my mind.
It didn't take hours and hours to find
Eight good lines are hard to do
So I put these rubbish two!

Sean McGrath (14)
Radyr Comprehensive School, Cardiff

River

A river is like a flowing dream
As subtle as a sleeping cat
Running down rocky mountains
Like a single tear.

A river is like a rippling piece of silk
Flowing in the wind
Of one person's dream
That will come true.

A river is a question
Where does it go
And where does it flow
Running into nothingness?

Stacie Nicholls (14)
Radyr Comprehensive School, Cardiff

Music

I like to listen to music,
It brightens up my day.
Pop, Rap, or R 'n' B,
It helps me on my way.

And when I'm feeling down,
Or had a dreadful day,
I just put on my headphones,
And my music I just play.

It calms me down when I am angry,
It makes me happy when I am sad.
It lifts my spirit when I am down,
It helps me all day through.

Claire Richards (13)
Radyr Comprehensive School, Cardiff

Game's Over

I'm waiting for you
I'm burning in the sun.
I can smell you
This must be fun.

I hear noises above me
They give me a fright.
I look up to see . . .
Magnificent things staring down at me
Oh my, what a sight.

Big round eyes
With a very sharp voice
They look pretty scary to me
Hand open ready to reach . . .
For me?

I try to get away from it
As fast as I can
But I could only hear it saying;
'This one looks cute!'

As I sit there wondering, scratching my head,
A hand makes a lunge for me!
'Oh no!' I cry
I turn onto my side
Pretending to be dead.
'Game's over pup'
It said.

Yeats Yeung (12)
Radyr Comprehensive School, Cardiff

The Hungry Horse

I am waiting for you,
In my lonely stable.
Surrounded by wooden boards,
Like a baby's cradle.

Kicking the door with all my might,
My boredom is growing.
I'll put up a fight,
Though it mightn't be showing.

Finally you arrive,
You've been setting up the jumping course.
Feed me! Feed me! Fast! Fast!
I'm a hungry horse!

Lucy Robins (12)
Radyr Comprehensive School, Cardiff

The Webbing

I am waiting for you
I have built my web
So hurry up so I can go to bed.

I am waiting for you
My dinner on wings
Is flying into my webbing.

I am waiting for you
You have come to me
And you are my tea.

I am waiting for you
I am a spider
You are a fly.

Robbie Scott (11)
Radyr Comprehensive School, Cardiff

I Am Waiting For You

I am waiting for you
Under the gate
I hear a car.
I jump out; I see it's not you
I go back under
I need a catnap
I am waiting for you.

My stomach is rumbling,
I see another me
I get my claws out
Ready to pounce.

I hear a car
I jump under again
I see you all
Calling me
I rub around your legs
I want you to feed me
Prrrrr!

Christina Sueref (12)
Radyr Comprehensive School, Cardiff

Football

I like football, it's the best,
Because it's better than the rest!
Davids, Ronaldo, Ronaldinho too,
They do the skill to try to beat you.
Football is like being in Heaven,
When watching Ronaldo the No 7!
I like football, it's the best,
The best sport, better than all the rest.

Adam Mackinnon (14)
Radyr Comprehensive School, Cardiff

Woof, Woof

I am waiting for you
To come on by
I am all alone
With one old bone.

I don't know whether to run
Or just glaze at the sun
I am getting very hot
Like I am boiling in a pot.

It is going to get dark
But I can still hear the other dogs bark
I am furry and fat
And I really love cats.

I hear the van coming
And a chubby man humming
At last I will have a home
I am no longer all on my own.

Hannah Bainbridge (12)
Radyr Comprehensive School, Cardiff

Just A Few Colours

These are just a few colours
A few colours that I can see
Blue, yellow, pink, green,
The colours that flow through me.

Crystal blue waves crashing down
A fiery sun setting behind a town
The pink growing heart of a girl's first love
A lush green meadow beneath the skies above.

Ida Hennius (14)
Radyr Comprehensive School, Cardiff

Kikanbo!

I'm waiting for you,
I hear your voice so clear,
The trees are poking in me,
I'm sure you'll find me here.

I'm waiting for you,
My heart is pounding fast,
My legs are quaking madly,
I pray you'll just walk past.

I'm waiting for you,
And your menacing spear,
You want to kill me,
Not caring about my fear.

I'm waiting for you,
I do not stand a chance,
You are a murderous fierce man,
I am just a small orang-utan.

Eluned Hyde (12)
Radyr Comprehensive School, Cardiff

The Maths Teacher

I opened the door dreading what I would find
A maths class inside
I wish I was blind
Or at the seaside
He stared as I sit down
I picked up my pen
I looked back and gave him a frown
And I said to myself, *'Shut up Mr Brown!'*

David O'Connor (14)
Radyr Comprehensive School, Cardiff

King Of The Jungle

I am waiting for you,
So I can have dinner.
Just get into view,
And I'll be the winner.

Hunting silently for food,
Deep in the wilderness.
I need to kill now,
To feed the lioness.

You are moving into sight,
I'm waiting for prey.
You can try all you like,
But you're not getting away.

I pounce on the antelope,
It has no chance.
I bring it to the ground,
My teeth like a lance.

I kill it on a rock,
Not pleasant to lie on.
But I'm the king of the jungle
I'm a lion!

Adam Heavens (12)
Radyr Comprehensive School, Cardiff

The Beach

The waves crash down on the shore,
The sand glistens under the gleaming sun.
Children build castles with buckets and spades
Adults sleep under the heat of the sun.

People surf in the clear blue water,
Others fly kites in the breeze.
Children run and jump and shout,
While their parents just lay about.

Daniel Coombes (13)
Radyr Comprehensive School, Cardiff

Hiding

I'm waiting for you
Waiting silently
Why are you here?
I smell you, you're not far
You're coming closer and closer.

Hunting quietly for me
I hide in the tree
So you can't see me
You pull the trigger
To warn me.

Searching in the jungle
Why are you trying to kill me?
What did I do to you?

I see you with your gun
You spot me in the tree
I try to run but it's too late
You've pulled the trigger and shot me
Bang!

Sophia Homayoonfar (12)
Radyr Comprehensive School, Cardiff

A Car

A car, a car can travel afar,
It can travel near, it can travel far.

A man named Clar drove the car,
So I said, 'Oi, Clar are you going near or far?'

Clar said, 'I'm going to the bar,'
So I said, 'Are you going to the near bar or the far bar?'
But by the time I said that, the light had changed green,
And Clar had gone off clean.

Ben Liguz (12)
Radyr Comprehensive School, Cardiff

Someone Take Me Home

Why are we waiting here
Looking out of the window?
Someone please be interested in us
We need some attention.

Someone to come and care for me
Any person who will pay for me
To pick me up
Put me in a box
And take me home.

We are all really cramped
All my brothers and sisters beside me
Lots of predators around me
Bigger animals all around
Someone get us out of this pet shop
Me and my hamster family.

David Walker (12)
Radyr Comprehensive School, Cardiff

Hiding In The Cupboard

I am waiting for you,
Hiding in the cupboard,
I'm ready to run,
Oh what fun.

I'm going to bite your tail,
Before your cheese goes stale,
All your hair,
Just like a bear!

I am waiting for you,
In my house,
Because you're a mouse,
You're so juicy and fat,
Lucky me, I'm a cat.

Ashley Blair (12)
Radyr Comprehensive School, Cardiff

Horsing Around

I am waiting for you,
To come to me,
You're really late,
And I want my tea!

I want to go see my friends,
And stuff my face with grass,
Oh hurry up now it's nearly
Quarter-past!

I'm really getting impatient now,
I'm starting to chew the door,
I'm getting really bored now,
Oh come on, it's nearly four!

I hear your voice call my name,
And I whinny back just the same,
I've been waiting all this time since two,
I'm your sweet little pony waiting for you!

Jessica Johns (12)
Radyr Comprehensive School, Cardiff

Pounce

I am waiting for you,
I know you will come,
I can't see you yet but I know you are there.

You are in the bush ready to pounce
I am keeping an eye open,
Ready for my prey.

So beware,
I have pounced,
The tiger has got you
In its claws.

Ellis Hodgson (12)
Radyr Comprehensive School, Cardiff

Horses Of The Forbidden Land

Horses,
Roaming wild and free,
Galloping among cloudy plains
Shrouded in mystery and doubt.
These are the horses of the Forbidden Land.

Horses,
White and cheerful,
Dancing to heavenly music,
Foals balancing on tiptoes,
Creeping through the dawn of time.
These are the horses of the Forbidden Land.

Horses,
Stunning as the land they live upon,
Fillies playing in-between forests of cloud,
Mares prancing through the beds of flowers,
These are the horses of the Forbidden Land.

Horses,
A new arrival appears,
Do not weep for him,
He is in a happy place,
Manes and tails flowing everywhere,
They come to greet him.
These are the horses of the Forbidden Land.

Beckie Drew (13)
Radyr Comprehensive School, Cardiff

The Constipated Dog!

There once was a dog,
That swallowed a log,
He needed the loo
But couldn't poo,
And that was the constipated dog!

He went to the chemist,
To buy a pill,
But the pill,
Made him
Really ill
And that was the constipated dog!

When he went to the loo,
He had a poo
Then the log
Came out in the bog
And that was the end
Of the constipated dog!

Rebecca Miller (13)
Radyr Comprehensive School, Cardiff

My Room

My room has the warmth of the sun
My room is a tranquil place
My room is my place of thought
My room is what my mind makes it
The sun shines through my windows like spears of light
This is the place I cherish
Although it changes it is the same
It changes every season
The place is mine
My own.

Gaël Shaw (14)
Radyr Comprehensive School, Cardiff

The Old Man And His Dog

The old man and his dog were sitting there,
The dog on the floor, the man on the chair.
The man had wrinkles; the dog had lots of long, wet hair,
But one thing in common, they were both sitting there.
On why, oh why were they sitting there?
Sitting there without a care.

The dog has a white and black coat and a long thin snout,
A big bushy tail and a loud vicious shout!

The old man with his overalls and flat dye cap
His turquoise jacket and his green boots which smelt of cow pat.

The old man and his dog were sitting there,
Sitting there like a contented pair.

Ben Montgomery & Jordan Osman (12)
Radyr Comprehensive School, Cardiff

Be Cool, Don't Go To School

School is not cool, don't be a fool.
How could it?
Stay at home and lay in bed,
It is much more fun, believe me, such fun.
Be cool, don't go to school,
Then you won't be a fool.
All the work? No way!
Lay in bed and go clear your head of all the work, work, work!

Alan Newton (12)
Radyr Comprehensive School, Cardiff

The Game

Walking through the stadium
It's a really big place.

The commentator speaking
Like God up above.

The crowd like a bunch of elephants
Running at a quiet pace.

Security guards looking round
Watching the crazy crowd.

Football players running fast
The crowd chanting with a blast.

Horns blowing at the end of the game
Yes, we won again!

Wales! Wales! Wales!

Lewis Hydes (13)
Radyr Comprehensive School, Cardiff

The Dragon

The dragon is the king of the sky,
He flies in the sky really high,
When he comes down to eat his prey
The little prey shouts out and says,
'I'm dead, I'm dead, I know I am!'
Then the dragon comes down
And eats him like he's roast ham.

Jack Shellard (12)
Radyr Comprehensive School, Cardiff

Still Having Fun!

Like a leaf
I grow from a seed
That slowly shoots up . . .

My golden brown hair
Waves in the wind,
And my bright eyes
Always shine
When the sunlight catches them.

I like to sing and dance
As I twirl in the breeze
And maybe some day
Travel the world,
Floating and soaring through the air
Without having to give a care.

Like a leaf
I hope that life will lead me
Down the right road . . .
And that I will still have fun
When I grow old!

Susie Reilly (11)
St Colombans College, Kilkeel

People Like This Should Get A Life!

People tell me what to do
Even though they don't have a clue.
People shout and people scream
But that's only because they are mean.
People give me mucky looks
I think these people totally suck.
They don't know what my life is like
So why can't they get out of it and take a hike?
If they could only see the best in me
Then I could live my life happily.
The pain inside is as sharp as a knife
These people should seriously get a life!

Alex Bainbridge (13)
St Hild's CE School, Hartlepool

Untitled

Life is fun,
Life is exciting,
Life is wild,
Life is enlightening.

Life is depressing,
Life is sad,
Life is boring,
Life is bad.

Life is . . .
How you want it to be
Through the eyes of the beholder
Life is free.

Faye Whitehead
St Hild's CE School, Hartlepool

What Am I?

It's as quiet as a newborn mouse,
And lives inside your house,
It's like a statue always sitting,
Staring almost glaring.

It lives under your bed,
And it's waiting to be fed,
Its black haunting eyes,
Like a midnight's sky.

Its sharp pointy claws,
Attached to its scrawny paws,
It's as round as a ball,
And not very tall.

It might speak,
If you take a peak,
Look at its big brown belly
Like a plate of jelly.

Take a light when you go and see
That your old teddy is unhappy.

Rachel Bell
St Hild's CE School, Hartlepool

Nursing Home

No one thinks I'm young and wise,
But I know I am deep down inside.
After my dinner you can see all my food,
All down my dress, some already chewed.
Is it my voice croaky and old?
Why don't you believe the things I have told?
I try so hard to do things for myself,
But I can't even put a book on a shelf.
So as I sit alone and still,
Look at me closer, promise you will?

Emily Winter (12)
St Hild's CE School, Hartlepool

Shall I Go To School Today?

When people make you feel down instead of up
And you don't know which way would be better to look.
You think it's better for it to be all bottled up inside,
And you think the best way out is suicide.

I stole some pills and thought about
Is this really the best way out?
So I went to school the next day
And told my teacher what I had to say.
And from that moment the bullying went away
And now I can go to school every single day
Without kneeling down and having to pray!

Sarah Coward
St Hild's CE School, Hartlepool

Imagine!

Imagine if we were all the same
Now wouldn't that be a shame?
You wouldn't be able to glow
And your true colours would never show.

Imagine a world of harmony and peace,
A world with no violence, no need for police.
No need for prison or punishment,
All the hatred we could prevent.

Imagine a world with no greed,
We could all write and read.
Together we would stand
All hand in hand.

Rachel Laybourn
St Hild's CE School, Hartlepool

My Brother, My Cousin And My Dad

My dad went to war the other day
My brother with him too
My nephew went along with them
I wonder what they'll do?

I heard they're in the trenches
My dad's got trench foot
Germans invaded the front line
Barbed wire they had to cut.

I hope someone shoots Hitler
Right through his puny brain
Again and again and again . . .

I remember when I was a little boy
Scared they'd never come home
Victory was served though
My brother, my cousin and my dad.

Liam Gray (13)
St Hild's CE School, Hartlepool

Me And My Mates

When me and my mates are out on a night
There's no need for chew, bullying or fights
Cos me and my crew are the best mates ever
Me, Sami, Elsa, Tasha and don't forget Emma.

Of course we have other cool mates as well
And with them there's no need to shout or yell
With Sammi, Jen, Jess, Lucy, Faye, Loz and Nadeen
And don't forget Jen Gant who is a total drama queen!

When me and my mates are out on a night
There's no need for chew, bullying or fights
Cos me and my mates are the best mates ever
And I hope to be mates with them forever and ever.

Emma Pounder (13)
St Hild's CE School, Hartlepool

Chav

They all stand in the corner with fags in their gobs,
Waiting for their mates, the 'Owton Manor Mob!'
They get in their cars, then off they go
To wait for some other chav to get their giro.

When the giro is cashed they all can get drunk,
Or go off to eat something which is usually junk,
They gang around the bus shelter all eating their chips
Or hang around the skate park giving the skaters lip!

They are cocky and mouthy and all have the same hair,
And their chavette girlfriends all have pushchairs,
They proudly show off their new camera phones,
They all play the same music, that Crazy Frog drone.

They have McDonald's for breakfast and chips for tea,
And they all love music and talk like Ali G,
When the giro is gone, they make their way home,.
To check on their pit bulls who have been left alone.

Robbie Wood (13)
St Hild's CE School, Hartlepool

Friends

Me and my friends go out on a night,
We laugh and carry on, but mostly play fight.

We go to the park; we go to the swings,
We go on the beach and do other things.

Build sandcastles, maybe paddle in the sea,
Skim little stones the size of a pea.

We watch the tide as it comes in,
Say bye to my friend who we call, 'Tin Tin'.

Now it's the end, time to go,
Say bye-bye I'll see you tomorrow.

Sophie Austwicke
St Hild's CE School, Hartlepool

Witch

Vanishing into thin air in a blink,
Appearing in placid places at night,
Forming things to grow or shrink,
They are witches in the flickering light.

Where she goes, nobody knows,
What she does, nobody can tell,
A wave of a hand as if to throw,
That is her magical spell!

That's why she appears at a crime,
And helps to get a criminal in a cell,
Flicker of her hands, she freezes time,
That is her magical spell!

As if she's prepared and knows what is going to happen,
She receives a vision - the future she can tell,
She deals out a good slapping,
That is her magical spell!

Andrew Townsend
St Hild's CE School, Hartlepool

Broken World

The sun slowly rises, fiery and bright,
I have never seen such an amazing sight.
The waves wash up on the rippling sand,
No one around, such a forbidden land.
Lush tropical trees sway gently in the breeze,
Not like at home where we all get a freeze.
So quiet and peaceful this land is
Beauty and tranquillity I will really miss.
This land is such a beautiful place
Shame it's being destroyed by the human race!

Laura Blackett
St Hild's CE School, Hartlepool

The Show Man

He sits in his dressing room, head in his hands,
He moves like a lion in foreign lands,
Inside his head a clock ticks and tocks,
On the outside, his body kicks and rocks,
He pulls on his gear and gets ready to go,
Cos he knows no one has got his flow,
His nerves are gone, erased from his mind
He copes with pressure, that you just don't find,
He steps on the stage, the crowd is roaring,
With each small step, his blood pressure's soaring,
All clad in white, from head to toe,
He plucks up the courage and grabs the mic,
And shows those people, a show they've never known like.
He looks at the crowd, his special omen,
Cos after all he is a show man.

Mark Austwicke (13)
St Hild's CE School, Hartlepool

Untitled

Red is a crimson rose . . . wilting,
Orange is the sun beaming down intensely,
Yellow is the golden sand scattered immensely,
Green is the lush grass . . . blowing in the wind,
Blue is the ocean glistening in the light,
Indigo is the heavenly sky, dark at night.

Natalie Mathieson
St Hild's CE School, Hartlepool

Poverty

No water
No food
No money
No home
But why?
Because of some loan
That's why
Have they paid their debts?
Yes, three times over
Then why are they still paying?
Who knows!

Rob Shearman (13)
St Luke's Science & Sports College, Exeter

The Man Under The Stairs

There's a man under the stairs
He only comes out at night
He creeps around the floorboards
And squeezes your wrists tight.

He never lets go
Until you wake up
And then he's gone.

'Where did he go?'
I hear you say
'Has he gone that far, far away?'

Well not exactly
Look under your bed
And there he will sit, scratching his head
He'll look at you in the strangest way
And you will not know what to say.

He'll visit you
Until you reach ten
And he'll never return again.

Jess Lind (12)
The Atherley School, Southampton

Isolation

I stand there isolated
Quiet and discontented,
They leave me out of
The fundraising event.

Just because I'm different
They laugh and tease,
I feel like I'm taking part
In the big freeze.

No matter what I say,
No matter what I do,
I'll always be willing
To have a friend like you.

The next day it was worse,
For the best though,
That day I saw God,
I was happy, I could glow.

Annaliese McGeoch (12)
The Ladies' College, St Peter Port

Witches

Cats, hats, brooms and bats
Witches are the funny sort
Thank goodness they are getting caught
Because they are so spooky
We all shout, 'Burn, burn, burn!'
Then, 'Let her churn . . . witch!'
They do weird spells
They throw cats down wells
Never in my life
Would I ever let my wife
Out at night for
The fear of a fight . . .
With the witches.

Katie Enevoldsen (11)
The Ladies' College, St Peter Port

Day Drifts By . . .

The morning has come
The night has gone
Dewdrops like pieces of glass
Hanging on the lush green grass
The bird sings its morning song
Its chorus lasts all day long
It stops and flies into the sky
And wakens a little butterfly
That goes to sleep behind the red flowers
To shelter from the summer showers
The morning sun raises its head,
The bright curtain around its head
The day draws on till the sun is high
The beautiful clouds drift gracefully by

Lorna Whattam (14)
The Ladies' College, St Peter Port

Blood Spill

You wipe away the tears,
That wash away your lies,
They burn away the mask you wear,
See the broken soul inside,
Your sullen eyes glow with your pain,
Your body fits and shakes,
A heart that's ripped and torn,
Stained by your mistakes,
So watch the blood spill softly,
Like rivers on your skin,
Falling like the crimson,
That takes away the sin.

Elizabeth Moffatt (14)
The Ladies' College, St Peter Port

The Bullies Of Manhattan

The bell rings.
People run and scream and sing.
The bullies crouch behind the wall,
Waiting, watching, until the small
New boy comes sliding past,
Expecting nothing. The bullies are fast.
They spring forwards and catch him
Round the neck and pull him in,
Like a fisherman reeling in his catch.

They take him hostage behind the bins,
Where the rats are picking food from the tins
Of beans that the cook's thrown out.
Everyone has gone home now without a doubt,
So the bullies can hassle the boy
For his hair and his glasses, here they feel joy.
Treating people like they were taught,
When they were little, when they fought,
The bullies of Manhattan School.

They dance their delight in the playground,
They dance on the sandpit mound.
The boy stands still, looking meek,
They hit him; he turns the other cheek.
They call him names and kick him,
Hit him until the lights start to dim.
Then his mum comes looking around,
The bullies hide and make no sound,
The new gang of Manhattan School.

Joanna Woodnutt (13)
The Ladies' College, St Peter Port

Just Believe

Walking through the mist of my mind,
Staring at the pale blue sky,
Can I leave my thoughts behind?
May I try?
Maybe if I just believe?

Gazing at the void of my guilt,
Screaming out my rage in distress.
What if I should wither and wilt?
What if I fail to impress?
Maybe if I just believe?

Falling in the pit of my despair,
Grasping for the iridescent light.
What if I should die, would I care?
Would I be able to muster the might?
Maybe if I just believe?

Pondering in the whirlpool of my sanity,
Wondering if I am in its heart.
Will I surrender to my vanity?
Will it tear my soul apart?
Maybe if I just believe?

Walking through the bars that make me free,
Staring at the ever pulsing light.
Did someone save me?
Can it be, I've won the fight?
It has saved me - just believe.

Alice Monaghan (13)
The Ladies' College, St Peter Port

The Loudest Silence

I'm living in a world that I can't understand,
I speak a different language, I talk with my hands.
All I've ever wanted is to fit in,
I'm still waiting for my life to begin.

All that I want is a little normality,
Something to restore what's left of my sanity.
To be accepted as the girl that is me,
Who can hear my desperate plea?

I am trapped alone in a foreign land,
Where all fun and laughter for me is banned.
I want to listen and I want to learn,
The silence just eats away and burns.

I have learnt to live, with just me,
But no one heard my silent plea.
I have coped with anger, I have coped with absence,
But pity is the loudest silence.

Kate Smith (13)
The Ladies' College, St Peter Port

Bullying

I hate the way you make me feel,
The way you make me scream.
I hate the way you pull my hair,
And the way you steal my dreams.

I hate the way you make me cry,
The way you push and pull.
I hate the way you make me angry,
And the way you make a sunny day dull.

But all in all I hate the way you make me scared,
And all muddled up inside.
I hate the way you bully me,
All I want to do is cry.

Ebby Mosgrove (13)
The Ladies' College, St Peter Port

The Witches' Spell

The witches surround a big round pot,
As the contents oils and gets hot.

They add what's needed to be fed,
And apply it as it's being read.

Add to water a cow's lung,
Stir it and then add a snake's tongue.

Later add a creature's jaw,
That's been lurking on the moor.

And a new trick, it will froth,
If you add a crisp, old moth.

As you watch it churn and turn,
Add a bat wing to make it burn.

Now that finally it is made
Serve and enjoy within two days.

Issey Norman-Ross (12)
The Ladies' College, St Peter Port

Dracula Is Dead

In the sun he crumples and dies,
Turning to dust before our eyes,
Once he was hurting, now he's dead,
He cannot kill you in your bed.

He is dead, before he was not,
His coffin will be left to rot,
Sucking your blood he was before,
He cannot do it anymore!

Tanith Cherry (12)
The Ladies' College, St Peter Port

The Haunted House

Sitting there in the middle of nowhere,
Deserted in a field,
Green lights flashing in a room
Faces at the window,
Broken glass on the floor
Blood splattered on the door
Bats flying round the house
Catching all the little mice
Little children's faces glow
Blood trickling very slow
Dracula sleeping in a coffin,
Now he's alive and gone missing!

Bella Chesney (12)
The Ladies' College, St Peter Port

Thanehood

(Inspired by Shakespeare's 'Macbeth')

Upon a desolate moor
Three hags stand
Deciding the fate
Of a powerful man.

They creep around the enchanted pot
Smoke unfurls green and gold
They speak of Thanehood
And another more ultimate goal.

Macbeth, Thane of Glamis
Thane of Caudor, hail the king!
Macbeth claims they're wrong
How could he be such a thing?

Niamh Hanna (12)
The Ladies' College, St Peter Port

Our Life In Four Verses

We enter the door to this world,
No destination or a map to guide,
Directors help us along the way,
Down the path we have chosen,
Just to end up all the same.

We walk along our road,
Finding and losing friends,
Together we laugh till we cry,
Always hard to say goodbye,
On these days we spend.

This journey is tiresome,
Take time to stop, sit and reflect,
On the memories we once had,
And hope they never fade,
These are times that we'll miss.

The door tries to seal itself shut,
Causes us to ask questions and never get answers.
Thoughts of passing bring upon us
The end of the line begins to blur
To find ourselves back to where we started from.

Chantal Marson (13)
The Ladies' College, St Peter Port

My Unusual Poem

This poem is unusual it's not like any other
It comes with a set of instructions,
A set of instructions that are strange and weird.

Don't forget to bring some food to put you in a really good mood.
Bring a bikini or something cool so you can go swimming in the pool.
If you need to go for a pee don't forget to go behind the tree.
If you want to stay up late, don't forget to bring a mate.
On my island you can have fun, take some suncream lie in the sun.

Alesha Solomon (12)
The Lakes School, Windermere

Survival

S is for the sun beating down on my back.
U is for the unbelievable heat on this island.
R is for reptiles coming around me at night.
V is for I am very, very hungry.
I is I need to keep going.
V is for I am very, very hot.
A is for adventure to the end of the Earth.
L is for life and it is worth living.

Robert Griffiths (12)
The Lakes School, Windermere

The Survival Poem

Every step I take the colder it gets
The snow, the wind, want me to rest
But I will keep on going, going till the end
When I reach it then I will rest
But I have not done my job yet.

Matthew Park (12)
The Lakes School, Windermere

I Will Survive

A normal bus journey
A normal train journey
A normal working day
But some people can't live with that.

Bang!
A bomb went off
Nine-thirty in the morning
Chaos all around.

Bang, bang!
Another six bombs went off
Injured people everywhere
Dead people everywhere.

Smoke and gas in the air
Debris and litter cover the ground
Emergency crew crowding around
London in distress.

Birmingham suffers too
Wedding parties destroyed
Evacuated bars, shops and hotels
Birmingham full of sadness.

The whole world thinks and prays for London
Al-Quaeda takes the blame
A tragedy strikes again
Where next?

Annie Garlick (11)
The Lakes School, Windermere

Bombs

Big Ben the clock
Tick-tock, tick-tock,
Everyone rushes,
To catch the Tube and buses.

Bang, bang! Two bombs go off,
Bang, bang! Two more, one on a bus,
The Tube and the station blown away,
Missing people, even today.

Scotland Yard are on the case,
But that doesn't make us feel safe,
The station walls are bust,
Everything wrecked, covered in dust.

Broken buses and trains,
People lying in pain,
Top of a bus blown away,
Forever we will remember this day.

Eilish Heatley
The Lakes School, Windermere

London Bombs

The cars are going
The trains are blowing
The people are calling
The walls are falling.

Cats are prowling
Dogs are growling
The city is in danger
Bombed by a stranger.

Tom Simmonds (12)
The Lakes School, Windermere

London

London was bombed on Thursday the seventh
Forty-nine people went up to Heaven.
The buses in the square were mangled and mashed,
While the trains in the Tube were horribly smashed.
Hundreds of people were wounded or killed,
The terrorists must think of the blood they've spilled.
The police have no idea of who planned the attack
But all know one thing, they will be back . . .

Christopher Hunter Marsh (12)
The Lakes School, Windermere

Africa Lives

In Africa one child every three seconds dies,
Is this the way they should live their lives?
For surely, no, this shouldn't be
It's not the same for you and me.

They are always hungry, they are always ill,
When they sleep at night, they feel the chill,
When we are all curled up at home,
Just remember they are all alone.

There are people that are normal and rich,
They will have a servant to scratch their itch,
But parts of Africa are wasting away,
Thousands more die each day.

So when you go to bed at night,
Remember the orphans scared with fright.
Who's to blame? It is a mystery,
We have got to *make poverty history!*

Rachel Pickup (14)
The Lakes School, Windermere

London's Bombing

L ondon on Thursday seventh July, a normal day until nine o'clock.
O n the London Underground, three bombs blew up on the
fragile trains.
N umber thirty bus driving along and *bang!* another bomb goes off.
D river on the bus survived the terrible attack.
O n the Underground, thirty-two people died on this terrible day.
N ever can this happen again.
B elow the busy London street unsuspecting people were going
to their fate.
O n the bus another seventeen people were awaiting their fate.
M en and women were screaming and wanting to get out.
B ombing that day was awful, it should never happen again.
I n the station it is quiet for the first time for a long time.
N o one should suffer from this awful day.
G oing to London will never be the same, never.

Will Britton (12)
The Lakes School, Windermere

Untitled

Normal London morning
People doing their thing
All of a sudden
People were woken
By several bangs
And smoke came out
Of the Underground tunnel
And the top of a bus blew off
Like throwing a shovel
Forty-nine dead.

Daniel Laffin (12)
The Lakes School, Windermere

Click

(This poem should be accompanied by the clicking of fingers in the relevant places)

Barely any water,
Barely any food,
Starvation putting life on hold,
A silent and solemn mood. *(Click)*

Sickness reaping precious lives,
With no contempt or guilt,
So terrible to die alone,
To fall asleep and wilt. *(Click)*

Children with no games or toys,
To keep them entertained
Such a different story here
But who is to be blamed? *(Click)*

Their health alone is awful,
They have the poorest aid,
But while we try to help them,
Our kindness is betrayed. *(Click)*

So whilst you have been reading,
Oblivious, unaware,
Prepare yourself, you will be shocked,
With what I am about to share . . . *(Click)*

Not just a petty sound or noise,
Each day the clock does tick,
The three seconds that each verse narrates,
A child dies for each click.

Ellie McKeown (14)
The Lakes School, Windermere

Surviving The Siula Grande Mountains

Joe falls and gets trapped
In a crevasse that is snow capped
He yelped
But he could not be helped.

He thought that he wouldn't survive
Until he felt an idea arrive
His ankle was throbbing with pain
He thought he was going insane.

Simon was safe at camp
Writing by a glowing lamp.

Stephen Gibson (12)
The Lakes School, Windermere

Survival Poem

London was bombed
On Thursday the seventh of July
The bombings killed forty-nine
Injured seven hundred at least.
There were four bombs
Three on the Underground
And one in a bus,
It must have been horrible to watch,
Hopefully that is the end.

Brandon Williamson (11)
The Lakes School, Windermere

In A Void

Void, cancelled, simply annulled.
Endlessly aching, unconsoled.
Life without meaning, cause without reason.
Touch without sense, time without season.

A shadowed face, anguished and marred.
An empty space, scaled and scarred.
Sweetly abiding to cynical charade.
Secretly hiding behind a fictitious façade.

Still, lost within this heart of glass,
This fragile and yet unfeeling mass.
Lies the remains of a love that glowed.
A gift to you I once bestowed.

But honour and pride now bereaved,
By your love for me so misconceived,
Ripped from my inner depths impending
Mind, body and spirit still bleeding.

A simple void, is that what I've become?
The hollow sphere on a pendulum.
Swinging back and forth, emotion to emotion,
Never stopping once, nor slowing the motion.
No reason, no answer, no justification.
The creation of a sterile imagination.
Just passing through time as time passes me.
Merely a nothing, a no one, to be.
Sightless and soundless, unseen and unheard.
Mindless and boundless, obscure and absurd.
All empathy lying, ungraced, unemployed,
I live my life dying, unembraced, in a void.

Holli Baker (15)
Torquay Grammar School For Girls, Torquay

Boring, Boring, Boring

There's nothing left for me to do
I'm bored with them
I'm bored with you
I'm bored with staying in my room
I'm bored with going shopping too
I'm bored with sleep
I'm bored in bed
I'm bored with all the food I'm fed
I'm bored out of my boring head
I feel as if I'm boring dead
I'm bored with clouds
I'm bored with rain
I'm bored with my computer game
I'm bored that everything's the same
I'm bored with being bored again
I'm bored with writing boring rhymes
About my boring, boring times
And so I'll finish . . .

Elliot Journeaux (12)
Wareham Middle School, Wareham

Weather

W et, rainy, thundering days
E erie clashing noise in May
A nd don't forget the lightning
T he lightning is very frightening
H earing rain pour in gutters
E ven my sister splutters
R ain, sun, clouds or fog, it's all to do with . . .

Weather!

Shannon Burbidge (10)
Wareham Middle School, Wareham

Ian Rush

This man is a true Kop legend,
On the pitch an all-time great.
He made the opposition push back and defend,
Scoring great goals was his lifetime fate.
He played his heart out in every match,
Making his opponents shell-shocked with fear.
Playing like a god; believe me there's no catch,
The number of goals he scored would cost the other team dear.
He had an amazing talent - you could say world class,
He would dribble the ball past all the rest.
Running up the pitch like he was late for Mass,
This Kop legend is the best of the best
Since then he's put on weight (but not as much as Uncle Fester)
And decided to manage small league club Chester.

Geoffrey Dragon (13)
Wareham Middle School, Wareham

Pets

Lots of different types of pets
On horses you can put on bets.
Greyhounds running round the track
To and fro they're coming back.
Rabbits running in the run
Looks like they're having fun.
Cats running round outside
When it's teatime they won't hide.
Guinea pigs squeaking in their cage
If they don't get dinner they go into a rage.
Hamsters round and round the wheel
Dried bananas they try to steal.
Go and buy pets in the pet shop
As long as they don't go . . . *pop!*

Paige Wallace (10)
Wareham Middle School, Wareham

Every Time

Every time I walk my street
The children seem to lack,
The power to look straight at me
And it's because I'm black.

Every time I walk my street
I look strangely back,
And the reason why they don't look at me
Is because I'm black.

Every time I go to school
I always sit at the back,
And when I ask why, they say,
'It's because you're black.'

Every time I go to the shops
I always go to the back
The reason why that happens is
Because I'm black.

Every time I see the memories
I always look back
I had a good life and the reason why
Is because I'm black.

Declan Walmsley (13)
Wareham Middle School, Wareham

Think

I can't think, I can't think
I just stand there and blink.

I can't think, I can't think
I just need to have a drink.

Connor Gordon (10)
Wareham Middle School, Wareham

Think

Coming at ten, I slip off serene
Coming at twenty, the bright light's a beam
Coming at thirty, I run off, I scream
Coming at forty, a killing machine.

My life has been stolen,
My family's joy too.
I lie on the tarmac,
My eyes stare at you.
The shock is not working,
My heart is a line
My family are watching
They stand there and pine

I want to be living,
I want to be free.
I need my mum round here,
To hug and hold me.
I want my dad here too,
A slap on the back.
To stop me from crying
When strength, I lack.

My soul it is ruptured
My family split too.
My heart has stopped beating
There's nothing to do.

So think when you're driving
Don't rush, slow it up.
But more to the point now
I'll never grow up.
Think!

Jessica-Rose Clark (13)
Wareham Middle School, Wareham

Equality At Last?

I have waited for a long time,
And the day has finally come.
We shall no longer be squashed
Under the white man's thumb.

Our race is given justice
And we now have our rights.
We are now just as equal
As the once all-powerful whites.

For once many years ago,
We were made enslaved.
For we were black and we were dirt
And freedom was richly craved.

The white men thought us demons,
Because of our dark skin tone.
They beat us and they flailed us,
And starved us to the bone.

But thanks to dear old Martin,
We blacks are finally free.
He brought us faith and justice
But his life became the fee.

But is there really justice?
Are we really free?
Will we now dine with white men?
That future is hard to see.

Even though there is a law passed,
That discrimination is no more.
That won't stop the white man
Beating us up on the floor.

Eleanor Wallace (13)
Wareham Middle School, Wareham

To Me And To You

I'm at the back no one will know how I feel all bottled up inside
My anger's rising no need to explain
No one cares for my feelings
I'm the only one who'll ever know that
There will be a way to my freedom
I will sit where I want on my local bus,
I won't fight for my seat.
I need my right to be one, no one telling I'm wrong cos I'm black
I don't want my life to be lived like that.

There will be a day when I will get the ice cream I want
No more of that leftover stuff.
Even though I'm at the front of the queue,
I wait and wait until my anger builds up again
I say, 'No thanks, I'll go. No need to waste my time on you.'

Today I sit in my seat,
I lick my ice cream I've always dreamed of,
I get the shoes I've never had the patience to buy
My rights I've got them at last,
Me and other black people will be forever treated the same.

Amy Derrick (12)
Wareham Middle School, Wareham

A Window

The possibilities are endless,
A view spreads far and near,
Cars drive past,
Birds fly gracefully,
Through the air, away to the clouds.

Outside is a landscape joyful and calm,
So near yet so far,
The window is a restriction,
From the inside to the out
Until I go I watch, I wait . . . I wonder.

Emily Rudd (13)
Wareham Middle School, Wareham

Your Help
(For Mother's Day 2005)

I would give you the sky but I couldn't wrap it
I would give you stars and the moon but I couldn't reach them
I would give you the sea but I couldn't hold it
I would give you the planets but I couldn't catch them
Then you came and helped
And we wrapped the sky and shared it
I sat on your shoulders and reached the moon and the stars
We held the sea together
Together we caught the planets
Without you I couldn't do it
Without your help to do it
Without your shoulders to sit on
Without your arms
Without you I couldn't do it
But you also gave me something I could never give back
You gave me my life and all your love
So I will give you my love too.

Kiri Snell (13)
Wareham Middle School, Wareham

A Recipe For A Night Out

Get a group of people
Add some nice clothes
Put them in a limo
Take the group from the limo and put into a club
Leave for a couple of hours
Pour on alcohol
And allow to soak
When all the group feel ill and can barely walk
Put the group back into the limo
And leave for a few minutes
Take the group back out of the limo again
Place the group into a flat
And let it sleep for at least eight hours but the longer the better!

Becky Fooks (12)
Wareham Middle School, Wareham

Kids

Five growing children
Sat on a wall,
One saw a mirror
He started to fall.

Four growing children
Playing with a hammer,
One hit a copper
Now he's in the slammer.

Three growing children
Hitting kids with sticks,
A gang gets involved
And hits them with bricks.

Two growing children
One weighs a ton,
Falls in a pool
Now there's one.

One growing child
Walking through a door,
Hinges give way
Now he's no more.

David Iles (12)
Wareham Middle School, Wareham

Football Poem

Chelsea are the richest club,
That's why they win it all,
With the chairman's money they buy,
Rooney, Becks and everyone else that's fly.
Every time they get the ball they always get a goal,
Lampard, Roben, Drogba and even Joe Cole.

Man United's been taken over by an American billionaire
If Arsenal aren't careful they'll get Ali Addiere.
They used to be the best
With every one of the greats taking it on the chest.

Liverpool are champions of Europe because they beat
All of the other greatest teams especially Chelsea's defeat.

Glen Strowbridge (12)
Wareham Middle School, Wareham

Dogs

There once was a dog that was sitting on a log.
He fell off the log and was bitten by a frog.
The frog did a jump and the dog grew a hump
The dog tried to jump and fell into a slump.

Tom McConnell (12)
Wareham Middle School, Wareham

Flying Over Africa

Tigers pouncing on their prey!
While monkeys keep out of the way.
Gorillas wish they could fly
Parrots fly high up in the sky.
The leopards run far away
Before the lion thinks it's prey.
The water is like a hot pan
Leaves, for monkeys are like fans.

Alex Lane (10)
Wareham Middle School, Wareham

Sport

Sport is played all over the world
Footballers are transferred, they are bought and sold.
Rugby players fight in lots of wars
Never choosing to ignore.

Golfers spend hours on their technique
Sprinters spend hours just to seek
World records, times to be smashed
Those times go by in a split second of a flash.

Sport players of all ages and sizes
Striving to achieve those big prizes
Throwing and kicking all types of balls
Sometimes looking cool, others like a fool!

Joseph Lillington (13)
Wareham Middle School, Wareham

Star Wars III

The spaceship of the Sith
Waiting for something to happen
Creeping through the darkness are clones
Attacking the Sith from behind.

The lightsabre battle commences
Beaming light penetrates the target
The noise is like thunder
Deafening all the way around them.

Anakin to the rescue
With a fighting weapon in his hand
He turns a beam into flashing red
All is destroyed
He has won
As he noticed he was Darth Vader!

Josh Terrar (10)
Wareham Middle School, Wareham

Liverpool Champions League Final

On the night, everyone was nervous
And as Gerrard walked onto the pitch,
I thought Milan were gonna kill us
And Milan were gonna put us into a ditch.

Their ancient captain Maldini scored after just one minute
And Milan knew they were gonna win it.
At half-time we were 3-0 down
And there looked to be no hope,
And Liverpool were gonna drown.

Gerrard scored and we had a chance
Smicer scored on his last appearance,
Liverpool were in a trance
And Traore made an amazing clearance,
Alonso scored from a rebounded penalty
And Milan crashed down to reality.

In the last minute of extra time
Dudek made a fantastic double save
From the greatest striker in the world
It would have gone in if it had curled.

It went to penalties and Shevchenko needed to score
But Dudek did a Grobbelaar and saved it
And the crowd let out a roar.

Gerrard lifted the cup, he couldn't believe it
Every Liverpool supporter hopes
He won't play next year's Champions League in a different kit.

Chris Cullinane (13)
Wareham Middle School, Wareham